Fungoes, Floaters and Fork Balls:

A Colorful Baseball Dictionary

Patrick Ercolano

Illustrations by Mike Lane

Prentice-Hall, Inc.
Englewood Cliffs, NJ

Prentice-Hall International, Inc., *London*
Prentice-Hall of Australia, Pty. Ltd., *Sydney*
Prentice-Hall Canada, Inc., *Toronto*
Prentice-Hall of India Private Ltd., *New Delhi*
Prentice-Hall of Japan, Inc., *Tokyo*
Prentice-Hall of Southeast Asia Pte., Ltd., *Singapore*
Editora Prentice-Hall do Brasil Ltda., *Rio de Janeiro*
Prentice-Hall Hispanoamericana, S.A., *Mexico*

© 1987 by

PRENTICE-HALL, INC.

Englewood Cliffs, N.J.

Library of Congress Cataloging-in-Publication Data

Ercolano, Patrick.
    Fungoes, floaters, and fork balls.

    1. Baseball—United States—Terminology.
2. English language—Slang—Dictionaries.   I. Title.
GV867.5.E69   1987   796.357′014   86-25306

ISBN   0-13-345075-9

PRINTED IN THE UNITED STATES OF AMERICA

For my mother and father,
with love and gratitude.

FOREWORD

by Red Barber

Patrick Ercolano's *Fungoes, Floaters, and Fork Balls: A Colorful Baseball Dictionary* is an easy book to read, but I'm sure it wasn't an easy one to write. The result of tremendous research, the book shows that the author, an experienced reporter, has combined his journalistic skills with his lifelong love of baseball, its stories, and its broadcasts.

I mention Ercolano's love of the game because, after all, you have to love something very much to do as much work as this book entailed. From every standpoint, this is the best baseball dictionary that I've seen. It is, as Casey Stengel used to say, "splendid."

But as good as this book is, it should become even better in later editions, thanks to the baseball fanatics who will pore over it. I know firsthand about the deep dedication of such fans. In my years of broadcasting ball games, I never made the slightest mistake—the flub of a fact, a figure, a name, or a date—that didn't immediately draw the ire of my most savvy listeners. So it will be that, despite the many entries in this book and the painstaking research that went into it, countless readers will write to offer arguments and, most important, additional words and phrases.

This is a fine piece of work, and I wish the author and his dictionary well.

ACKNOWLEDGMENTS

Many people were generous with their advice and encouragement while I worked on this book. Each of them has my deepest appreciation. I especially would like to thank four gentlemen whose assistance and willingness to help were, to use a sports cliché of recent vintage, "awesome." They are Red Barber, the Babe Ruth of baseball broadcasters; Rex Barney, the former Brooklyn Dodger fireballer and now the public address announcer at Baltimore's Memorial Stadium and a commentator on telecasts of Baltimore Oriole games; Robert Creamer, for three decades a writer and an editor at *Sports Illustrated*; and Harold Rosenthal, who has covered baseball and other sports for New York newspapers since the 1940s.

Thanks also to Paul Ercolano, Ron Ercolano, Bruce Lenes, Lisa DeNike, Jenny Abdo, Lou Niss, and the staff of the Library of Congress in Washington D.C.; to my MVPs (Most Valuable Proofreaders), Vincent Ercolano, John Fairhall and John Scholz; to my editor at Prentice-Hall, Tom Power; and to Liza Kirwin, without whom it wouldn't have been.

INTRODUCTION

On the final day of the 1984 regular season, Mike Witt of the California Angels pitched a perfect game against the Texas Rangers. The next morning Witt appeared on a national television program and described what he was thinking during the game, particularly in the ninth inning. One thing he didn't want to do, he said, was to throw any "cookies" to the Texas batters.

In homes across America, countless viewers unfamiliar with baseball and its vernacular must have scratched their scalps and tried to picture Witt winging Lorna Doones or Oreos toward his opponents.

Witt's use of the word "cookies" illustrates two points. First, many baseball expressions are associated with food. Offhand I can list "pepper," "tomato," "can of corn," "tater," "pea," "apple," "pretzel," and "mustard." No wonder people are always eating at the ballpark.

Second, and probably more important, is this: Baseball has a vast and colorful language that, in number and flavor of terms, outdoes the vocabulary of any other American sport. For evidence I submit the roughly 1,500 entries in this book, many of which ("strike out," "make a hit," "rhubarb," "touch base," "hardball," "ball game") have spilled over into common parlance.

Baseball is by nature a talking game, its gradual pace and pastoral setting lending itself to conversation. Words flow in the dugout, around the batting cage, in the press box, in the radio and TV booths, and in the stands. Did the pitcher bring his good stuff today? Has the cleanup hitter's sore wrist healed? Will the plodding right fielder be replaced in the late innings? Is the blonde in the box seat alone? All these matters, and more, are grist for gab during a game.

Numerous sources have supplied baseballisms over the years, but most have been coined by players, reporters, and broadcasters. While watching a game from the dugout, writing an account of a game, or describing it for the airwaves, there are only so many times you can say that a player "hit a home run" before the act begs for a new description. Why not say he "dialed 8," "took the pitcher deep," "juiced one"? A bat is a bat is a bat, but it is also a "wand," a "war club," a "mace," a "piece of iron," a "morning journal," a "banana stick," a "pole." Mike Witt could have said he didn't want to give the Texas batters any easy pitches to hit, but instead he served up "cookies."

Granted, some of these linguistic inventions are less memorable than others; we could probably learn to live without "stanza" and "canto" for "inning," or "orchardman" and "pasture worker" for "outfielder." The great coinages, however, possess the ring of poetry—"frozen rope," "humpback liner," "Gashouse Gang," "tools of ignorance," "circus catch," "paint the black," to name a few. It's no coincidence that baseball is the game preferred by those with literary leanings, the game that inspires the bulk and the best of the serious writing about sports. Indeed, the language of baseball contains many of the elements that appeal to lovers of words—vibrancy, humor, and tradition.

Especially tradition. Our oldest native sport, baseball connects us to our past. The game's lingo is part of that connection. When we call a pitcher an "ace," we automatically, if not knowingly, link him to Asa Brainard, the Cincinnati Redleg pitcher who notched all 56 of his team's wins in 1869. Every "at bat" is tied to the game in which the term was first used, an 1872 exhibition in Belfast, Maine, between a local nine and the Boston Red Stockings. Every "Texas leaguer" arcs back to the late 1800s, when the term was originated by a Toledo sportswriter.

This book is for Everyfan, from the green beginner to the seasoned diehard. The beginner, I trust, will benefit from the definitions of the most basic terms and enjoy, along with the diehard, the derivations and the historical information provided in many of the entries. I set out to produce the most comprehensive and entertaining baseball dictionary available. I hope you find that I met my goal.

And yet, as Red Barber suggests in his foreword, some of you might want to start a rhubarb with me over certain sections of the book. Someone will undoubtedly find a favorite term missing or know of a definition variation that I overlooked. After all, baseballese, like any large and expanding language, is nearly impossible to gather in total. I would be happy to hear from anyone who has a suggestion or a beef. I'm following the example of a good umpire, who is perfectly willing to listen to a well-presented argument, so long as it doesn't get personal.

Patrick Ercolano

> You can look it up.
> —Casey Stengel

ace: n. 1. An excellent pitcher. The term usually refers to a team's best starting pitcher, although it may also pertain to the best reliever on a pitching staff, as in BULLPEN ACE or RELIEF ACE. "Ace" derives from Asa Brainard, the only pitcher on the Cincinnati Red Stockings team of 1869. Brainard's record, as well as the team's, was 56 wins, no defeats, and one tie. Thereafter, any pitcher who won many games was called an "Asa," which was eventually shortened to "ace." Also STOPPER. 2. A run. In the 1840s, when the first amateur baseball teams were being formed by men's recreational clubs, card terms were often applied to baseball, such as "ace" for a run scored.

action pitch: n. A pitch thrown on a count of three balls and two strikes with two outs and a man on first base, men on first and second, or with the bases loaded. In any of these situations, the man or men on base start running just before the pitch is thrown, so as to get a jump in case of a base hit.

afterpiece: n. The second game of a doubleheader. Also NIGHTCAP.

agent: n. A representative hired by a player to handle his business affairs, especially contract negotiations. In 1970 baseball team owners agreed that a player could use a representative in salary negotiations. Three years later Jerry Kapstein became the first agent under the new system. His first client was outfielder Richie Zisk of the Pittsburgh Pirates.

air ball: n. A fly ball, a baseball term of the late 1800s.

Alibi Ike: n. A player who has an excuse for every one of his failures on the field. The name comes from a 1915 Ring Lardner short story of that title about such a player. See CLUB-HOUSE LAWYER, JAKE, JAKER, and PEBBLE PICKER.

alley: n. The area of the outfield between the left fielder and the center fielder, or between the center fielder and the right fielder. Also GAP and POWER ALLEY.

all over the plate: adj. Unable to throw strikes. The phrase refers to a pitcher whose deliveries are consistently and variously out of the strike zone, and may also refer to the pitches themselves. Also WILD.

All-Star break: n. The three-day break in the regular season during which the All-Star Game is played.

All-Star Game: n. An annual exhibition game pitting the best players of the American League against the best of the National League. Also MIDSUMMER CLASSIC. In 1933 *Chicago Tribune* sports editor Arch Ward conceived the idea of the game, which would be played at Chicago's Comiskey Park in conjunction with the city's Century of Progress exposition. The game took place on July 6, with Babe Ruth's two-run homer leading the Americans to a 4-2 win. Selection of the All-Star squads, always a controversial process, was decided by the respective managers (the skippers of the previous season's league champions) through the 1946 game, although fans offered their suggestions in informal polls taken by baseball officials in 1933 and 1934. From 1947 to 1957, the selection was handed over to the fans. But after Cincinnati rooters were accused of stuffing the ballot box in favor of Red players in 1957, major league players, coaches, and managers began picking the All-Star teams, and did so through 1969.

Baseball commissioner Bowie Kuhn returned the vote to the fans in 1970. Two All-Star Games were played each season from 1960 through 1962.

alternative pitch: n. A euphemism for an illegal pitch. When a pitcher is having a bad game, he often has no alternative but to go to his bag of tricks, the most useful of which is illegally putting some foreign substance—such as hair cream, saliva, or sweat—on the ball, so as to make it break sharply and unexpectedly as it nears home plate. See DOCTORED BALL.

American Association: n. 1. A professional baseball league that lasted from 1882 through 1891. It was the third major league formed, after the National Association (1871–1875) and the National League (1876–   ). 2. One of the three minor leagues at the top, or AAA, level of the minors, along with the Pacific Coast League and the International League.

American League: n. One of the two major leagues, the other being the National League. Abbreviated AL. Also JUNIOR CIRCUIT. The American League was founded in 1901 by Byron Bancroft "Ban" Johnson and immediately proclaimed itself an equal competitor of the National League, which had been founded 15 years earlier. The new league was dubbed the "junior circuit," a name that is still used even though the two leagues have been considered equals from the early years of their rivalry. The AL's charter member teams were in Baltimore, Boston, Chicago, Cleveland, Detroit, Milwaukee, Philadelphia, and Washington, D.C. In 1969 each major league was restructured into two six-team divisions known as the Eastern and Western Divisions. In 1977 the American League added one team to each of its divisions.

angel: n. A cloud, in a virtually cloudless sky, that allows a fielder to better see a high fly ball. Also GUARDIAN ANGEL.

Annie Oakley: n. A base on balls. Complimentary tickets to the theater or to sporting events have traditionally been punched with holes to designate that the tickets are free. During the late 1800s, these freebies were called "Annie Oakleys" in honor of the famous riflewoman whose feats included shooting holes in small cards. Baseball observers quickly adapted "Annie Oakley" to mean a base on balls, which was and still is also known as a "free ticket" or a "free pass."

ant: n. A fan. The word dates from the early 1900s and stems from the observation that fans in the stands often appear as small as ants to the players (and, to some players, as insignificant as ants).

appeal play: n. A special appeal made by the defensive team to an umpire after a baserunner has failed to tag up on a fly ball or has neglected to step on a base while advancing or while returning to his original base. To put out the runner on an appeal, a defensive player with the ball must tag the runner or the base he missed or the base from which he failed to tag up properly. The appeal must be made to the umpire before the next pitch. The umpire may have seen the misplay but will not call the out unless appealed to by the defense.

apple: n. A baseball, so called for its resemblance to an apple.

arbiter: See UMPIRE.

arbitration: n. The process by which an objective party, or arbitrator, settles a contract dispute between a player and the management of his team. Such arbitration cases are binding; the ruling is entirely in favor of either the player or the club. Arbitration was first used in major league baseball in 1974.

Arlie Latham: n. A sharply hit ground ball that is difficult to field. A major league third baseman during the late 1800s, Arlie Latham had a reputation for letting hard grounders go by rather than risk injury by getting in front of them.

arm: n. 1. Outstanding throwing ability, as in "This young shortstop has a lot of arm." 2. A strong throwing arm. Also BAZOOKA, CANNON, GUN, and RIFLE.

around the horn: prep. phrase. Refers to a double play in which the third baseman fields a ground ball and throws to the second baseman, who forces a runner at second base and then throws to the first baseman to retire the batter. The term derives from the custom of ships to take the long route around Cape Horn at the tip of South America to get from the Atlantic Ocean to the Pacific Ocean, or vice versa, before the construction of the Panama Canal.

artificial turf: n. A synthetic, carpetlike surface that has replaced the grass fields in some major league stadiums. Also CARPET and RUG. The first artificial playing surface was installed in the Houston Astrodome in 1965. On April 9 of that year, the New York Yankees beat the Houston Astros, 2–1, in an exhibition at the Astrodome, the first game played on a synthetic surface. The best editorial comment about artificial turf came from a player—often attributed to either Willie Mays or Dick Allen—who remarked, "If cows don't eat it, I won't play on it."

ash: n. A bat. Because of its resiliency and strength, ash has long been one of the favored types of wood for the manufacturing of bats.

aspirin, aspirin tablet: n. A baseball thrown or pitched with such great speed that it appears as small as an aspirin.

assist: n. A credit for a fielder's direct involvement in a put out. He gets an assist by making a throw that results in a put out, or by touching a batted ball in a play that results in a put out.
    v. To make an assist.

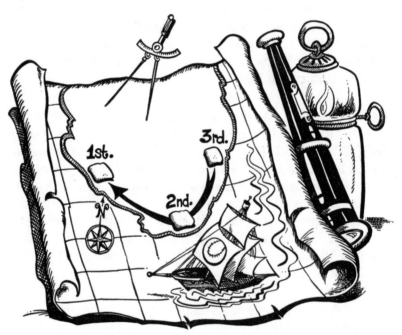

AROUND THE HORN

at bat: n. An official batting turn. A batter is not credited with an at bat if he gets a base on balls, makes a sacrifice, is hit by a pitch, or is interfered with or obstructed by a defensive player. Abbreviated AB.

    prep. phrase. Taking a batting turn. Also UP.

    "At bat" was first used in an 1872 game in the seaport town of Belfast, Mass., where a local nine was playing the Boston Pilgrims. A sailor keeping score would announce to the crowd of seamen and their families, using familiar nautical terms, that the current hitter was "at bat," the next was "on deck" and the one after him was "in the hold" (the "hold" being the interior of a ship). The latter phrase evolved into "in the hole." In the mid-1800s, when some baseball terms were borrowed from card games, an at bat was called a "hand."

atom ball: n. A ball hit sharply and directly at a fielder, or right "at 'em." The phrase can also be spelled "at 'em ball."

away: adj. 1. On the road, playing a game, a series of games, or more than one series in the opponent or opponents' home stadiums. 2. Outside of the strike zone, on the side of the plate farther from the batter. Also OUTSIDE.

ATOM BALL

backstop: n. 1. The fence behind home plate, which prevents batted or thrown balls from going into the stands. 2. See CATCHER.

bad-ball hitter: n. A batter who often makes base hits by swinging at pitches that are out of the strike zone. Former New York Yankee catcher Yogi Berra and Roberto Clemente, once a Pittsburgh Pirate outfielder, were notorious bad-ball hitters.

balk: n. An illegal motion by the pitcher that, once detected by an umpire, allows the baserunner or runners to advance one base. Generally resulting from the pitcher's failure to follow through on his delivery to the plate or on a pick-off attempt, a balk is called by any of the umpires when the pitcher

1. Makes any motion associated with his pitch and then fails to make a delivery, while touching the pitcher's rubber with his foot;
2. Bluffs a throw toward first base and then fails to make any throw, while touching the rubber with his foot;
3. Fails to step directly toward a base while throwing to that base, while touching the rubber with his foot;
4. Throws or bluffs a throw to an unoccupied base for a

purpose other than making a play, while touching the rubber with his foot;

5. Makes an illegal pitch;
6. Throws a pitch to the batter while he is not facing the batter;
7. Makes any motion associated with his pitch while not touching the rubber with his foot;
8. Delays the game unnecessarily;
9. Bluffs throwing a pitch when he doesn't have the ball and while standing on, astride, or completely off the rubber;
10. Removes one hand from the ball after coming to a legal pitching position, for a purpose other than making a pitch or a throw to a base;
11. Accidentally or intentionally drops the ball while touching the rubber;
12. Pitches when the catcher is not in the catcher's box, while giving an intentional base on balls;
13. Delivers the pitch from his set position without coming to a full stop.

Enacted in 1898 and revised two years later, the balk rule was written primarily to prevent pitchers from using deceptive motions to pick off baserunners.

ball: n. 1. A pitch thrown out of the stike zone. When a pitcher has thrown four "balls," the batter is awarded first base, or a "base on balls." In the 1800s, a ball was called a "wide" because the pitch was outside, or wide, of the strike zone. See BASE ON BALLS. 2. The ball used in the game of baseball. See BASEBALL.

ball-and-strike umpire: See UMPIRE-IN-CHIEF.

ball had eyes, the: An expression referring to a slow, bouncing ground ball that barely eludes two infielders, as if the ball saw the fielders and deliberately bounced past their reach. See SEEING-EYE HIT.

ball hawk: n. An aggressive fielder, one who tries to reach as many batted balls as he can. The term usually is applied to a speedy outfielder, particularly a center fielder who tends to range all over the outfield in pursuit of fly balls.

balloon pitch: n. A slow, high-arcing pitch. Also BLOOPER PITCH, BUTTERFLY, EPHUS, and LALOB.

ballpark, ball yard: n. An enclosed field or stadium where a baseball game is played. The first ballpark was Brooklyn's Union Grounds, built in the early 1860s. The wooden ballparks of the late 1800s proved to be fire traps, so during the early twentieth century concrete and steel were used to both reinforce old parks and construct new ones. Among the steel-and-concrete structures erected in the early 1900s were St. Louis's Sportsman's Park in 1902, Philadelphia's Shibe Park and Pittsburgh's Forbes Field in 1909, Cleveland's League Park and Chicago's Comiskey Park in 1910, Brooklyn's Ebbets Field, New York's Polo Grounds and Washington's Griffith Field in 1911, Boston's Fenway Park, Cincinnati's Crosley Field and Detroit's Tiger Stadium in 1912, Chicago's Weeghman (later Wrigley) Field in 1914, and Boston's Braves Field in 1915. Later developments included the erection of lights for night baseball in 1935, and the first artificial surface and the first dome stadium in 1965.

Baltimore chop: n. A batted ball that hits near home plate and bounces so high as to allow the batter to beat the throw to first base. The term originated with the National League Baltimore Orioles of the 1890s. Led by players such as John McGraw and Wee Willie Keeler, the Orioles would purposely swing down, or "chop," at pitches in order to produce the high-bounding hits. Such a grounder is still sometimes called a "Baltimore chop," although the player of the modern era, with its lively ball and emphasis on power hitting, rarely

BALL HAWK

makes a deliberate attempt to bat the ball into the ground. Also BOUNDER, BUTCHER BOY, CHOP, CHOPPER, and TOPPER.

banana stick: n. A bat made from bad wood—a hitting instrument, it was said, as effective as a banana. Also MORNING JOURNAL. Compare PIECE OF IRON.

band box: n. A baseball stadium with small interior dimensions. Boston's Fenway Park and Chicago's Wrigley Field (also known as "The Friendly Confines") typify the band box, and in fact are the remaining examples of the old-style homey baseball ballparks.

bang-bang play: n. A put-out or attempted put-out in which a runner and the ball arrive simultaneously at a base or at home plate. Also BING-BINGER.

banjo hit: n. A batted ball that results from a weak swing. The term was coined in 1924 by a minor league second baseman named Ray "Snooks" Dowd, who observed that such a hit makes a sound like a strummed banjo string—"plunk."

banjo hitter: n. A batter who has little or no power. See BANJO HIT. Also JUDY and PUNCH-AND-JUDY HITTER.

barber: n. 1. A pitcher who often throws pitches that come close to or "shave" the batter. Also HEADHUNTER. 2. A pitcher with excellent control, one who can throw pitches that pass over or "shave" the corners of home plate. Sal Maglie, a pitcher who started out with the New York Giants in 1945, was nicknamed "The Barber" for both his habit of throwing pitches close to batters and his outstanding control. 3. A garrulous player. The name derives from chatty barbers (the tonsorial type). Waite Hoyt, a talkative pitcher who played from 1918 to 1938, was the first player to be so labeled.

BANG-BANG PLAY

barnstorming tour: n. An extended tour during which base-ball players travel from town to town and play either among themselves or against a local team. Such tours, now virtually extinct, were undertaken to earn extra money for players and to promote big league baseball. "Barnstorming" derives from a term originally used to describe rural tours by itinerant theatrical troupes, who would perform one day in a small hall or a barn and then hastily "storm" to another town for the next day's performance. Baseball's first barnstorming tours came in the 1870s, when American professionals played in Ireland, England, and Cuba. During the next 30 years, there were tours all around the world, with the first trip to Japan occurring in 1908. A Japanese barnstorming tour by U.S. stars in 1931 drew about 250,000 people to four games, and is credited with starting Japan's love affair with baseball. From 1918 to the 1950s, a major league team would usually con-clude its spring training by barnstorming with another team up the east coast, traveling in trains that would stop in vari-ous towns where games would be staged. But with the advent of air travel and because the practice of barnstorming by train became too costly, the tours declined drastically after the Second World War. Every few years, however, a major league team goes on a playing tour of Japan.

base: n. One of the four points on a baseball diamond, marked with a 15-inch square canvas bag at first, second, and third bases, and with a five-sided rubber plate at the home base, or "home plate." The bases are set 90 feet from each other and secured to the ground. The intention of the team at bat is to score runs by starting at home plate and advancing counterclockwise around the bases until returning safely to home. The defensive team can make outs by tagging a runner as he attempts to advance to a base or by forcing him out at a base. During baseball's early days, wooden stakes signified the game's bases, a concept borrowed from the English game of rounders. Later the stakes were replaced by flat stones, which by the mid-1800s were removed in favor of small sacks much like the canvas bases used today. Also BAG, HASSOCK, and SACK.

baseball: n. 1. A game played by two nine-member teams (ten-member teams in games that use the designated hitter—that is, in almost all games outside the National League) on a field bordered by two foul lines that form a V-shaped, 90-degree angle. Opposite this angle is, theoretically, infinite space, though most fields come equipped with a fence about 400 feet away from the angle. At the point of the angle is home base or home plate. Down the right foul line, 90 feet from home plate, is first base. Ninety feet from first base, on a straight line with home plate, is second base, and third base is 90 feet from home plate on the left foul line. The tilted square formed by the bases is called the diamond, also known as the infield. The part of the field beyond the infield and between the foul lines is the outfield.

The game is played with one team positioning nine defensive players, or fielders, on the field, while the other team sends one man at a time to home plate, where he stands with a bat that he uses in trying to hit a small round ball thrown by a member of the defensive team called the pitcher, who stands on a ten-inch high mound 60 feet, six inches from home plate. The other defensive players are the catcher, who squats behind home plate and wears protective gear on his face, chest and shins; the first baseman, positioned near first base; the second baseman, between first and second bases; the shortstop, between second and third bases; the third baseman, near third base; the left fielder, on the left side of the outfield; the center fielder, in the middle of the outfield; and the right fielder, on the right side of the outfield.

The defensive team's objective is to cause the offensive team to make three outs and no, or at least few, scores, better known as runs. On the other hand, the offensive team hopes to score runs by advancing their players counterclockwise around the bases to home plate. A run is scored each time a player safely crosses home plate. Methods of getting on base are the base hit, the base on balls, being hit by a pitch, reaching base because a fielder made an error on a play, reaching base after the third strike has eluded the catcher, and being interfered with by the catcher while batting. To record an out, the defensive team can strike out a batter, catch a ball that has been batted into the air, or field a ball that has been batted onto the ground and throw it to a defensive player who is touching a base before the batter or a baserunner reaches the base. When three outs have been recorded, the other team bats until it has made three outs. After both teams have batted, an inning is completed.

Games usually last until the team with the fewer runs has batted in nine innings. If the score is tied after nine innings, then extra innings are played. If the visiting team (the team that batted first) scores in extra innings, it must allow the other team to bat and keep it from tying or going ahead in the score to win the game. But if the home team (the team that batted second) breaks a tie in extra innings, then the game is immediately over and the home team wins. When inclement weather or darkness forces a game to be stopped and the losing team has batted for at least five full innings, then the team that is ahead in the score wins the game. The offensive team may have coaches stand in the field in defined areas in foul territory (any part of the field not contained within the foul lines) near first and third bases. Officials called umpires are stationed at each base and are responsible for making rulings on each play and the general conduct of the game. The home plate umpire rules on whether pitches are balls or strikes, and is the ultimate authority in each game.

Baseball is considered to be the national sport of the United States, although it is played in nearly 100 countries. The game is said to derive from the English sports of cricket and rounders. Primitive versions of baseball known as One Old Cat, Two Old Cat, and "town ball" reportedly were played by Americans in the 1700s. Baseball began taking its modern form in the mid-1840s when a New York bank teller named Alexander Cartwright laid out the diamond and wrote the game's first rules. Over the years the word also has been spelled "Base Ball," "base ball," and "base-ball," and is said to have first appeared in "A Little Pretty Book," published in London in 1744, specifically in a poem called "Base Ball." It goes: "The Ball once struck off/Away flies the boy/To the destin'd Post/And then Home with Joy." The author is un-known.

2. The round, white ball with raised stitches, which is used in the game of baseball. With a cork center wrapped in twine, a ball measures about nine inches in circumference and weighs about five ounces. In 1974 cowhide replaced the traditional horsehide as the exterior material of a baseball. Also APPLE, ASPIRIN, ASPIRIN TABLET, HORSEHIDE, LEATHER, PEA, PILL, POTATO, ROCK, SEED, and TO-MATO. See DEAD BALL and RABBIT BALL.

v. To play baseball. "Baseball" was used as a verb in the 1800s, though virtually no one uses it in that sense today. If anyone did, he would get some pretty funny looks.

baseball Annie: n. A baseball groupie, a woman who seeks out the company of professional ballplayers. Also GREEN FLY.

baseball card: n. A small card that usually features a baseball player's photograph on the front and his career statistics on the back. The cards are sold in packs with pieces of bubble gum. Also BUBBLE GUM CARD. The first baseball cards were printed on paper and appeared about 1880 in packs of Old Judge, Piedmont, Sweet Caporal, Polar Bear, and Recruit cigarettes. Bubble gum cards, made of cardboard and larger than the cigarette cards, first appeared in 1933 and remain popular to this day, though production was halted during World War II. The most valuable baseball card is the 1910 Honus Wagner card produced by Sweet Caporal. When Wagner, a nonsmoker, learned that he had posed for a tobacco company, he ordered that all the cards be removed from circulation. Only seven are known to have survived the call-back, and each is valued at $1,500. An estimateed 1.5 billion baseball cards were produced in 1984, up from 500 million in the late 1970s.

Baseball Writers Association of America (BBWAA): n. A national organization of American baseball journalists. The BBWAA was founded in 1908 by a group of disgruntled baseball writers who decided to form a united front in trying to obtain better working conditions at World Series games. By vote among its members, the BBWAA has decided the Most Valuable Player Award since 1931, the Cy Young Award since 1956, and the Rookie of the Year Award since 1947. The organization also votes on Hall of Fame inductees.

base hit: n. A batted ball that allows the hitter to reach a base safely without virtue of an error by the defense. Also BASE KNOCK.

base knock: See BASE HIT.

base on balls: n. The awarding of first base to a batter after the pitcher has thrown him four pitches out of the strike zone, or "balls." Baseball officials ruled in 1877 that a batter would not be charged with an official time at bat when he has received a base on balls. Between 1880 and 1887, the number of balls for a base on balls was changed from nine to eight to seven to six to seven again and to five, before four was finally settled on in 1889. Also ANNIE OAKLEY, FREE PASS, FREE TICKET, FREE TRIP, PASS, TICKET, and WALK.

baserunner: n. An offensive player who has reached a base by a walk, a hit, an error, being hit by a pitch, being interfered with by the catcher, or running to first base safely after the catcher has dropped what would have been the third strike. The baserunner's fervent hope is to advance to every base until he reaches home plate and scores a run. Also MAN and RUNNER.

basket catch: n. A catch of a fly ball, made by holding the glove palm up like a basket and at stomach level. While New York Giant outfielder Willie Mays popularized the basket catch in the 1950s, Rabbit Maranville, a National League shortstop from 1912 to 1935, is said to have been one of the first players to make the play regularly. Also BREADBASKET CATCH and VEST-POCKET CATCH.

bastard pitch: n. A pitch that is thrown to such a location that the batter is unable to hit the ball and is left muttering, "That pitch was a real bastard!" or "That pitcher is a real bastard!"

bat: n. The wooden cylindrical instrument used by offensive players to hit a pitched baseball. The modern bat, thicker at the top (or "head") than at the handle, measures 30-plus inches in length and 30-plus ounces in weight, and up to 2¾ inches in diameter at the head. The heaviest bat used in modern times was Babe Ruth's 54-ounce model; the longest, a 38-incher belonging to Al Simmons; and the shortest, Wee Willie Keeler's 30½-inch bat. The first bats used in baseball were flat-sided cricket bats. In 1862 it was ruled that baseball bats had to have a rounded surface, but not until 1893 were flat-sided bats banned altogether. For the 1880 season only, four-sided bats were allowed. Over the years bats have been made of wood from willow, hickory and ash trees and even old wooden wagon tongues. Nowadays, however, most bats are made from ash. Also ASH, CLUB, HICKORY, LOUISVILLE SLUGGER, LUMBER, MACE, POLE, STICK, WAGON TONGUE, WAND, WAR CLUB, WHIP, WILLOW, and WOOD.
    v. To take a turn at bat.

bat boy: n. A uniformed, nonplaying member of a team, usually a boy in his teens, whose various duties include doing errands in the clubhouse, picking up and putting away players' bats during games, and keeping the on-deck circle supplied with the materials a player might need while preparing to take his turn at bat, such as towels and pine-tar rags. The home team generally has its own regular bat boy and provides one to the visiting team. Until about 1920, a bat boy was known as a "mascot," and was often a man with a physical deformity.

Bat Day: n. A promotion in which baseball bats are given free to young customers at a game. Maverick baseball owner Bill Veeck ("as in wreck") is credited with staging the first Bat

Day. During the 1951 season, when he was owner of the St. Louis Browns, Veeck received 6,000 bats from a manufacturer on the verge of bankruptcy. After pondering how one goes about unloading 6,000 baseball bats, the resourceful Veeck hit on the idea of giving them away to young fans at a Browns home game.

bat rack: n. A multisectioned rack that hangs on each team's dugout wall and contains players' bats. In some stadiums the bat racks are large bucketlike containers that sit on the dugout floor. Also WOODPILE.

batsman: n. The batter. In the mid-1800s some baseball terms, including "bat" and "batsman," were borrowed from cricket, primarily because Henry Chadwick, the first person to write about baseball in depth, was an Englishman and an avid fan and chronicler of cricket before becoming fascinated by America's new sport.

batter: n. The member of the offensive team who is at bat. Also BATSMAN, CUTTER, HITTER, STICK, STRIKER, and SWINGER.

batter's box: n. The rectangular area drawn on either side of home plate, in which the hitter stands while batting. Each box measures six feet long and four feet wide and is parallel to and six inches from the side of the plate. If the umpire sees that the batter has any part of either foot outside of the box while hitting the ball, the batter will (or should be) ruled out. Many batters try to prevent this embarrassment by using their feet to wipe away the outline of the box, which is drawn with white chalk or lime. With no lines, particularly no back line, the hitter can stand deeper in the box, have a longer look at the pitch, and be less susceptible to a warning from the ump to stay inside the box.

battery: n. A team's pitcher and catcher during a game. Dating from the 1860s, when it initially referred only to the pitcher, "battery" is said to derive from military parlance. Just as one soldier hands ammunition to the soldier who fires an artillery battery, so does the catcher signal which pitches the hurler must "fire." Baseball reporter Henry Chadwick wrote in 1889 that the pitcher and catcher are to a team "what the battery of a regiment is to the line of infantry." See OCCUPY THE POINTS.

batting average: n. A statistic that reflects a player's success as a hitter, based on the ratio of his base hits to his at bats. To figure a batting average, divide base hits by at bats. Batting average, abbreviated BA, is the basis of each major league's batting champion; the player with the highest BA wins the crown. Baseball reporter Henry Chadwick began computing a primitive form of the batting average in the mid-1860s, figuring the ratio of hits to games. On August 10, 1874, Boston baseball writers started tabulating BA in its current form.

batting glove: n. A snug-fitting glove, essentially a golf glove, that a player can wear while batting to get a better grip on the bat. The slugging New York Yankees of the 1950s are said to have introduced the batting glove (perhaps to protect their hands from the chafing caused by hitting so many home runs). Now players like to slip on special gloves not only for hitting but also for protection while sliding hands-first into a base and for added cushion under a fielding glove.

batting helmet: n. A plastic cap that a player wears to protect his head while he bats. Some catchers wear them for extra protection while in the field. Roger Bresnahan, a catcher for the New York Giants, wore the first batting helmet at bat in 1907, shortly after he had been seriously injured by a pitch to his head. The helmet, named the "pneumatic head protector" by designer A.J. Reach Company, looked like a football helmet that had been sliced down the middle; the batter wore it on the side of his head that faced the pitcher. In the early 1950s, Branch Rickey, general manager of the Pittsburgh Pirates, ordered all his players to wear plastic batting helmets.

Although their new hats initially brought them ridicule (one writer dubbed the helmeted Bucs "Rickey dinks"), other batters around the majors were shortly modeling the latest in plastic headwear. Even so, most players didn't wear helmets until the American League made them mandatory in 1957 and the National League did the same soon thereafter. After Boston Red Sox outfielder Tony Conigliaro was almost killed by a pitch to his head in 1967, some teams added plastic earflaps to their helmets.

batting order: n. The numbered order of how the nine players who are participating in a game will bat. Also LINEUP. A manager tries to arrange his batting order with quick players who often get on base in the first two slots, the more powerful hitters in the three through six slots, and the weaker hitters in the seven through nine slots. In games that include designated hitters, there are still only nine slots in the batting order, but the player being batted for by the DH (almost always the pitcher) can be said technically to be part of the "line up."

batting-practice fastball: n. A derisive name for a weakly thrown fastball. The term refers to the slow and intentionally hittable pitches served up during batting practice.

batting stance: n. The stance a hitter takes while standing at the plate and awaiting a pitch. For definitions of the three types of batting stance, see CLOSED STANCE, OPEN STANCE, and PARALLEL STANCE.

bazooka: n. A strong throwing arm. Also CANNON, GUN, and RIFLE.

BB: n. 1. Abbreviation for base on balls 2. A ball thrown or batted with such great velocity that it appears as small as a BB.

bean: v. To throw a pitch, usually deliberately, that hits a batter. See BEAN BALL. Compare BRUSH BACK.

bean ball, beaner: n. A pitch that hits, or "beans," the batter. A pitcher usually throws a bean ball with the intention of hitting the batter, to avenge either a previously hit batsman from the pitcher's team or an offensive outburst by the team at bat. Also RAWLINGS LOBOTOMY. Compare BRUSHBACK PITCH.

bees in the bat: n. A stinging sensation in a batter's hands. It usually results from his not holding the bat tightly enough when hitting the ball, or from hitting the ball in chilly weather.

bench: n. 1. The players on a team other than those in the starting lineup, so named because they spend most of the game sitting on the bench in the dugout or in the bullpen. 2. The bench in either the dugout or the bullpen.

bench player: n. A reserve player, who spends a lot of time sitting on the bench. The tag carries with it a certain derision, though bench players can take heart from the bromide that says a team is only as good as its bench, or something like that.

bench jockey: n. A team member who, from his seat on the dugout bench, taunts the umpires or members of the opposing team. The bench jockey—so named because he insults or "rides" his opponents—is believed to have originated with John McGraw and the Baltimore Orioles of the 1890s, a feisty team that had many methods for unnerving the other club. Probably the champion bench jockey of the modern era was Leo "The Lip" Durocher, a player and a manager in the major leagues for nearly 50 years. Bench jockeying has virtually disappeared from the game, thanks in part to the increase in college-educated athletes and the advent of union solidarity among players.

benchwarmer: n. A reserve player, who spends much time "warming" or sitting on the bench during games.

BENCH JOCKEY

bender: n. A curve ball, which "bends" on its way to the plate.

Berraisms: n. The comical and yet inherently wise utterances credited to Yogi Berra, the catcher for the New York Yankees from 1946 to 1963, and later a coach and a manager with both the Yankees and the New York Mets. Among the most oft-quoted Berraisms are

- "How can you think and hit at the same time?"
- "In baseball, you don't know nothin'."
- "If you can't imitate him, don't copy him."
- "You mean right now?" (when asked for the time)
- And probably the best-known Berraism of all, "It ain't over 'til it's over." This phrase sums up not only baseball but also life itself, which was undoubtedly Yogi's intention when he made the remark.

big bill: n. A ground ball that takes a high and easily playable bounce toward the bill of the fielder's cap. Also CHARITY HOP and GRAVY HOP.

big inning: n. An inning in which the offensive team scores three or more runs in its at bat.

big league: n. One of the two major leagues. In the late 1800s, when the National League was the only major league, it was known as "the Big League." When the American League was founded in 1901, 15 years after the National, the term became "Big Leagues." Other leagues that were "major," if not as long-lived as the American and National, were the National Association (1871 through 1875), the American Association (1882 through 1891), the Union Association (1884), the Players' League (1890), and the Federal League (1914 and 1915).

adj. 1. Of or relating to the major leagues. 2. Of top rank or quality, as in "That was a big league catch." Also MAJOR LEAGUE.

big team: n. A major league team. The "big team" is what a minor league player aspires to. Variations include "big club," "big shew," "big show," "big time," and "the bigs."

bing-binger: See BANG-BANG PLAY.

bingle: n. A base hit, generally a single. The word dates from the early 1900s and is said to be a hybrid of "bingo" (a term for a base hit from baseball's early days) and "single."

bird dog: n. A part-time scout who "hunts down" baseball prospects in limited geographic regions.
    v. To stand slightly behind a baserunner while he is taking his lead, just to let him know that a pick-off play is possible.

black: n. The black-painted boundary of home plate. A pitch that passes over this area is said to "hit the black" or be "on the black."

Black Sox Scandal: n. A famous baseball scandal in which eight players for the Chicago White Sox—Joe Jackson, Lefty Williams, Chick Gandil, Swede Risberg, Fred McMullin, Happy Felsch, Buck Weaver, and Eddie Cicotte—conspired with gamblers to deliberately lose the 1919 World Series between Chicago and the Cincinnati Reds. Williams and Cicotte were the pitchers of record in all of Chicago's losses in the best-of-nine Series won by the Reds in eight games. Cicotte later admitted taking a $10,000 bribe. When the scandal became public at the end of the 1920 baseball season, American League president Byron Bancroft "Ban" Johnson ruled that all eight players would be barred from baseball for life. A ninth major leaguer, St. Louis Browns second baseman Joe Gedeon, was also banned from the game because he bet on the Reds after learning about the fix. The Chicago players who weren't accused in the scandal—or, as the contemporary press called them, the "Square Sox," "Opposite Sox,"

"Clean Sox" and the "lily whites"—were each given $1,500 bonuses by team owner Charles Comiskey. That amount, he reasoned, was the difference between the winners' and losers' shares in the Series. It was during the height of the scandal that a young boy, a White Sox fan, reportedly spotted Jackson in public and uttered the now-famous expression, "Say it ain't so, Joe!"

blank: v. To shut out, particularly to pitch a shutout. A pitcher "blanks" the other team when he allows no runs.

blazer: See FASTBALL.

Bleacher Bums: n. The self-named band of Chicago Cub fans who specialize in raising a ruckus in the bleachers of Chicago's Wrigley Field while rooting on their heroes. The term reportedly was first used in the late 1960s when it was applied to the rowdies who drank rivers of beer, wore yellow hard hats, and mercilessly jeered the Cubbies' opponents.

bleachers: n. Customer seating usually located behind a ball-park's outfield wall. Bleachers—also known as "bleaching boards" as far back as the late 1800s because of their exposure to sunlight— typically are the least expensive and least comfortable seats in the house.

bleeder: n. A sarcastic name for a bloop fly or slow ground ball that becomes a base hit. It's known as a "bleeder" because someone, usually a member of the opposing team, will facetiously say the ball was hit so hard that "the bat is bleeding." Invariably someone else will add, "Wipe the blood off that bat."

bloop: v. To hit a bloop or blooper. See BLOOP (n.).

bloop, blooper: n. A batted ball that falls toward the area of the outfield between the infielders and the outfielders. Also DYING QUAIL, FLARE, LOOPER, QUAIL, QUAIL SHOT,

TEXAS LEAGUER, and WOUNDED DUCK. Compare PARA-
CHUTE.

blooper pitch: n. A slow high-arcing pitch, generally intended
to cause the batter to pop up. Also BALLOON PITCH, BUT-
TERFLY, EPHUS, and LALOB.

blow it (the ball) by the batter: v. To throw a fastball past the
batter's late swing.

blue darter: n. A sharply hit line drive through or over the
infield, a batted ball as straight and hot as a blue gas flame.

bonus baby: n. A talented young amateur player who has
been given a large cash bonus to sign a contract with a professional baseball team. After the introduction of the amateur
draft in the late 1960s, young nonprofessionals had to sign
with the teams that drafted them or else go through the draft
again the following year. Previously, however, a talented
young amateur could sign with the highest bidder. In 1948
pitcher John Antonelli, who went on to a long career in the
majors, signed his first contract for a bonus of $65,000. The
first bonus baby was Dick Wakefield, who received a $52,000
contract from the Detroit Tigers upon his graduation from
the University of Michigan in 1940.

book, the: n. Information on a particular player's tenden-
cies, based on observations of his past performances. If a
pitcher knows from experience that a certain batter can't hit
a high fastball, then that detail becomes part of the pitcher's
"book" on that batter.

Book, The: n. The unwritten rules of thumb for how the
game of baseball should be played. For instance, The Book
decrees that a runner on second base not run to third base
when a ball is hit to the left side of the infield, or that a no
balls-two strikes pitch be thrown out of the strike zone, or
that a third baseman play near the left field foul line and well

behind third base during the late innings of a close game. Most managers follow The Book, though a select few depend more on intuition. As veteran manager Dick Williams said in 1980, "I never play by The Book because I've never met the guy who wrote it." Also PERCENTAGE BASEBALL.

boot: v. To make an error—in particular by literally kicking a ball while trying to field it. Also KICK.
n. An error.

bottom of the inning: n. The second half of an inning, during which the home team bats.

bouncer: n. A ground ball that takes a few moderate bounces.

bounder: n. A high-bouncing ground ball. Also BALTI-MORE CHOP, BUTCHER BOY, CHOP, CHOPPER, and TOPPER.

boxman: n. A pitcher, so dubbed because in the late 1800s, before there were pitching mounds, a hurler worked from a triangular box. See PITCHER'S BOX.

box score: n. A chart that condenses much of the information from one baseball game, such as the statistics for each batter and pitcher, the overall hitting and pitching stats for each team, errors, the number of baserunners left on base by each team, home runs, stolen bases, wild pitches, and so on. The first box score appeared in the *New York Herald* on October 25, 1845. Partly describing the previous day's contest between two teams from New York and Brooklyn, this box score listed only "hands out," or the number of outs each batter made, and the runs each batter scored. New York won the game, 37 to 19.

bread-and-butter pitch: n. A pitcher's best pitch, the one most effective in getting out batters. Also OUT PITCH.

breadbasket catch: n. See BASKET CATCH.

breaking ball: n. A curve ball whose flight "breaks" downward as it nears home plate.

break the wrists: To bring the top wrist over the bottom wrist while swinging at a pitch. When a batter tries to hold up a swing, the umpire determines whether the batter "broke his wrists." If so, then a strike is called; if not and if the pitch is out of the strike zone, then a ball is called. Also COMMIT ONESELF, GO AROUND, and PULL THE TRIGGER. Compare CHECK SWING.

break with the rubber: v. While pitching, to remove the back foot from the pitching rubber after reaching a set position.

bring it: v. To make a pitch or a throw, particularly a pitch, that has great velocity.

broken-bat hit: n. A base hit that causes the bat to break upon contact with the ball. Most hits of this type are soft liners over the infield or slow ground balls.

brush back: v. To throw a pitch purposely near or at a batter without intending to hit him. A pitcher "brushes back" a hitter for various reasons; he may be avenging a brushback or knockdown pitch previously thrown at one of his teammates, retaliating for an offensive outburst by the other team, or trying to move back a batter who is standing close to the plate. Pitcher Sandy Koufax of the Los Angeles Dodgers once said, "Pitching is the art of instilling fear." Also DUST, DUST OFF, KNOCK DOWN, SPIN THE BATTER'S CAP, and STICK THE BALL IN THE BATTER'S EAR. Compare BEAN.

brushback pitch: n. A pitch thrown near or at a batter, without the intention of hitting him. Also CHIN MUSIC, DUSTER, GILLETTE, KNOCKDOWN PITCH, and PURPOSE PITCH. See BRUSH BACK. Compare BEAN BALL.

Brush Rules, The: n. The basic rules for conducting the World Series, set in 1905 by New York Giants owner John T.

BRUSH BACK

Brush. When the Giants won the 1904 National League pennant, he refused to send his team into a postseason series against the American League champion Boston Red Sox. In Brush's opinion, the Red Sox represented a minor league (even though the Boston Pilgrims of the American League had won the first World Series, played in 1903). After much public outcry over his decision, Brush relented the following season and agreed to let his pennant-winning Giants face the Philadelphia Athletics in the 1905 World Series. First, however, Brush stipulated that the Series be run according to certain rules he had written. They have been refined over the years, but the Brush Rules remain the core of Series logistics, including the playing of a best four-of-seven set of games and the limiting of the postseason roster to players who were on the major league club before September 1. Also JOHN T. BRUSH RULES, THE.

bubble gum card: See BASEBALL CARD.

bug: See ANT.

bug on the rug: n. A batted ball that takes one or more high bounces on an artificial-turf field. The phrase reportedly was coined circa 1970 by Pittsburgh Pirates radio announcer Bob Prince.

bullet: n. 1. A sharply hit line drive. 2. A fastball.

bullpen: n. 1. The area of the ballpark, either in foul territory alongside the outfield foul lines or just beyond the outfield fence, where players, especially pitchers, warm up before and during a game. 2. A team's staff of relief pitchers.

Among the numerous theories for the origin of "bullpen," the most popular (and credible) explanation is that the term derives from the Bull Durham tobacco advertisements that covered the outfield walls of most turn-of-the-century ballparks. Pitchers often warmed up deep in fair territory next to the signs that displayed a large drawing of a bull. Theory number two: In common parlance, the word means a

BUG ON THE RUG

makeshift prison. Thus in 1909, when Philadelphia Athletics manager Connie Mack started the custom of having his pitchers warm up in a separate and secluded area of the field, "bullpen" was offered as a natural name for the enclosure. The third theory: Some baseball historians claim that the word has its root in the sport of bullfighting. After one bull has been killed in a bout with a matador, the bullpen gate is opened and another bull is led out. Similarly, when a pitcher has been knocked out of a game, a relief pitcher is called from the bullpen. Still another theory (number four) holds that Bill Friel, an infielder-outfielder for the American League Milwaukee Brewers of 1901 and a former railroad worker, introduced the word to baseball. When rail employees took a break, they would sit beside the roadbed on a bench called the "bullpen." While with the Brewers, Friel once observed a group of pitchers sitting on a bench in foul territory and, recalling his railroad days, dubbed the area the "bullpen." Or so the story goes.

bullpen ace: n. A team's best relief pitcher. See ACE.

Bums: n. A nickname for the old Brooklyn Dodgers. The name originated during the Depression when one particularly irate Dodger fan took to standing in the first row behind home plate at Brooklyn's Ebbets Field and cursing the inept home team. The fan showed a special fondness for the word "bums." It caught on, and stuck even through the Dodger dynasty years following the late 1940s. By then "Bums" or "Dem Bums" had become more of an affectionate tag. When the Dodgers moved from earthly Brooklyn to glitzy Los Angeles in 1958, somehow "Bums" did not fit the team's image any longer and fell into disuse.

bunch the batter up the middle: v. To defend a particular batter by positioning the fielders closer than usual to the middle of the diamond. This alignment is used against batters who tend to hit the ball up the middle.

bunt: n. A slow ground ball, most often rolling no farther than the pitcher's mound, that the batter makes by lightly pushing his bat at a pitch or by allowing a pitch to hit his bat. The bat is usually held motionless and about parallel to the batter's belt.

    v. To make a bunt.

    "Bunt" is a corruption of the word "butt," which was used to describe the hit because a bunt is made with the butt end of a bat and also because the occasional pushing motion with the bat resembles the way a goat or a ram uses its horns to butt an object. Although Dickey Pearce of the Brooklyn Athletics is credited with introducing the bunt in 1866, it did not become a widespread ploy until a decade later when Tim Murnane of Boston's National League club often used a flat-sided bat to "butt" the ball. See also DRAG BUNT, SACRIFICE BUNT, SQUEEZE BUNT, and SWINGING BUNT.

bush league: n. A minor league. Also "bushes."

    adj. 1. Of or relating to a minor league. 2. Lacking style or integrity. Also "bush."

    In standard (that is, nonbaseball) language, "bush" means "uncultivated country." Thus, as far back as the turn of the century, the word was applied to the small, mostly rural towns where minor league teams were located. In addition, the word "busher" could be either another name for a minor league player or a derisive term for a major leaguer.

bust the batter inside with a fastball: v. To throw a fastball close to a batter, especially around his chest.

butcher boy: n. A high-bounding ground ball. New York Yankee manager Casey Stengel coined this term, reasoning that a batter who hit such a grounder had to swing down on the ball as a butcher would chop down on a piece of meat. Also BALTIMORE CHOP, BOUNDER, CHOP, CHOPPER, and TOPPER.

butterfly: n. A slow, high-arcing pitch, particularly a knuckle ball, whose flight seems as delicate as a butterfly's. See KNUCKLE BALL.

Cactus League: n. The unofficial name for the major league teams that encamp in Arizona and California for spring training. Compare GRAPEFRUIT LEAGUE. See SPRING TRAINING.

calcimine: See KALSOMINE.

can of corn: n. A fly ball that can be caught easily for an out. The term is traced to turn-of-the-century grocers who stored canned goods on high shelves. To get one of the cans, a grocer would push it off the shelf with a stick. The can would then fall easily into his hands.

cannon: n. A player's throwing arm, particularly a strong arm. Also BAZOOKA, GUN, and RIFLE.

canto: n. An inning. In general parlance, a canto is a division of a long poem.

carpet: n. An artificial playing surface. Also ARTIFICIAL TURF and RUG.

Cartwright, Alexander: n. The man who is credited with being the father of modern baseball. For years it was believed that Abner Doubleday invented the national pastime, but later research uncovered Cartwright as the man who established the game much as we know it. A surveyor and a teller at New York's Union Bank, Cartwright organized the first modern baseball game and set many of the basic rules that remain the core of the game's structure. In that first game, Cartwright's Knickerbockers lost 23–1 to a team called the New York Nine on June 19, 1846, at the Elysian Fields in Hoboken, New Jersey. Cartwright designed the diamond, set the bases 90 feet apart, established teams of nine players each, and ruled that each side would bat until it made three outs. See DOUBLEDAY, ABNER.

"Casey at the Bat": n. Ernest Lawrence Thayer's poem about Casey, the mighty Mudville slugger who struck out to end a crucial game. Probably the most famous literary work about baseball, "Casey" first appeared in the *San Francisco Examiner* on June 3, 1888, under the byline "Phin." Many a fan of the game can recite whole verses of the poem, especially the final stanza:

> "Oh, somewhere in this favored land the sun is
>   shining bright,
> "The band is playing somewhere, and somewhere
>   hearts are light;
> "And somewhere men are laughing, and some-
>   where children shout,
> "But there is no joy in Mudville—Mighty Casey has
>   struck out!"

See DO A CASEY and PULL A CASEY.

catch: v. 1. To grab a ball that is in flight. 2. To play the position of catcher.
    n. 1. The grabbing of a ball that is in flight. 2. A nickname for the catcher.

catcher: n. 1. The defensive player positioned behind home plate, usually in a squatting position, and whose duties include catching pitches thrown by the pitcher and signaling to the pitcher what type of pitches should be thrown. The catcher wears protective gear such as a face mask, a chest protector, and shin guards. He also uses a large round glove. Also BACKSTOP, CATCH, and RECEIVER. 2. The position played by the catcher.

catcher's box: n. A rectangular area behind home plate, measuring four feet wide and extending six feet behind the back line of the batter's box. The catcher must stay inside this box until the pitcher throws the ball.

catcher's interference: See INTERFERENCE.

catcher's mask: n. A protective mask made of steel bars, padded where it touches the catcher's face and held on by straps that fit over the head. The home plate umpire wears a similar mask. Also FACE MASK and MASK. Jim Tyng, a catcher for Harvard's baseball team in the mid-1870s, was the first man to wear a mask. It was designed for him by team-mate Fred Thayer, who had a Boston tinsmith cut eyeholes in a fencer's mask and then added some padding to the chin and forehead areas to keep a foul tip from driving the mask onto the catcher's face. Thayer devised the mask after noting that Tyng's fear of having balls hit his face was causing him to lose confidence behind the plate. Tyng first wore the mask in an April 1877 game in Lynn, Massachusetts. Shortly there-after Jim "Deacon" White of the National Association be-came the first professional player to wear a catcher's mask after he developed one made of steel wire bars and padding.

catcher's mitt: n. A large round fielding glove worn by the catcher. One section of the glove contains the thumb, the other contains the four fingers, and a strong leather web con-nects both sections. The front, or palm side, of the mitt is heavily padded except at the center, or pocket. Although the padded catcher's mitt did not come into widespread use until the early 1890s, three men claimed to have previously invented the modern mitt. Independent League catchers Doug Allison and Nate Hicks each said they first used the large mitts around 1870, while Jim "Deacon" White of the National Association asserted that his padded buckskin glove of 1872 was the prototypical catcher's mitt. In any case, until the 1890s most catchers merely padded the standard flimsy fielder's mitt with materials ranging from goose feathers to raw meat. See FIELDING GLOVE.

caught leaning: adj. phrase. To be put out in a pick-off at a base while leaning toward the next base. This happens to baserunners who take too big a lead and are caught by a quick throw from the pitcher just before he would deliver to home plate or from the catcher immediately after the pitch.

caught stealing: adj. phrase. Tagged out while attempting to steal a base. Abbreviated CS. The "caught stealing" statistic was kept on an unofficial and sketchy basis from the mid-1800s until 1920, primarily by newspaper writers and editors. Even after 1920, when the major leagues began keeping official count of the stat, there were seasons when officials of both leagues decided it was not worth tabulating. The National League has counted the stat from 1920 to 1925, and from 1951 to the present. With the exception of 1927, the American League has kept track of players caught stealing from 1920 to the present. According to these official figures, the player who holds the all-time season record for most times caught stealing is Rickey Henderson of the Oakland A's, who was caught 42 times in 1982, the same year he set tha all-time season record for steals with 130.

cellar: n. The bottom spot in the standings, where the last-place team in a league or a division resides.

center, center field: n. 1. The middle area of the outfield, between left field and right field. 2. The position played by the center fielder. 3. A nickname for the center fielder.

center fielder: n. The defensive player who is positioned in center field. The center fielder generally is the fastest and the best of the three outfielders, and is responsible for directing movement in the entire outfield. Also CENTER, CENTER FIELD, and MIDDLE GARDENER.

chain: n. A group of minor league teams owned by a particular baseball organization. See MINOR LEAGUE.

Chalmers Award: See MOST VALUABLE PLAYER AWARD.

championship season: n. The regular season, the games that determine the champion of a Division or, as in the seasons before the Divisional format was begun in 1969, a league.

chance: n. An opportunity for a defensive player to make a put out by fielding a batted ball or making a throw that would retire a baserunner.

change, change of pace, change-up: n. A pitch that travels slower than what might be expected from the motion used by the pitcher. For instance, on a "straight change," a pitcher uses his fastball delivery motion but throws a pitch that travels much slower than a fastball; in other words, a slow fastball. On a "curveball change," a pitcher uses his normal curveball motion but throws a much slower curve. The change-up is designed to disrupt the timing of the batter's swing. Also LET-UP PITCH and OFF-SPEED PITCH.

charity hop: n. A high, easy-to-field (and thus charitable) final hop of a ground ball. Also BIG BILL and GRAVY HOP.

charley horse: n. Soreness or stiffness in a leg muscle. According to H.L. Mencken's *The American Language*, Supplement II, the term can be traced to baseball. One theory is that "charley horse" comes from the name of Charley "Duke" Esper, a major league pitcher of the late 1800s who supposedly had the gait of a lame horse. Another theory says the term derives from a horse named Charley that was part of the groundskeeping crew at a Sioux City, Iowa, ballpark in the late 1800s.

chart: v. To keep a pitch-by-pitch record of a pitcher's performance during a game.
  n. See PITCHING CHART.

chatter: n. Encouraging words, usually for a pitcher or a batter, hollered by his teammates on the field or in the dugout.

check swing: n. A swing that the batter abruptly tries to stop about halfway through his swinging motion. If the umpire rules that it was a check swing and if the pitch was not in the strike zone, then the pitch is called a ball. Also HALF-SWING. Compare BREAK THE WRISTS, COMMIT ONESELF, GO AROUND, and PULL THE TRIGGER.

cheese: n. A fastball, so called because it has a lot of zing, like a spicy cheese.

chest pad, chest protector: n. 1. A protective vestlike padding worn on the front of the catcher's torso and held by straps that wrap around his back. 2. A padded cushion that the home plate umpire holds outside the front of his torso or wears inside his shirt. Umpires used the handheld outside protector until the 1970s, when the inside protector, said to afford more comfort and maneuverability, became the choice of nearly every ump. Chest protectors were first worn by catchers and umpires alike around 1885.

Chicago: v. To shut out a team. There are two theories for this term's origin. First, on June 23, 1870, a Chicago team was shut out, and because blankings were rare occurrences in those days, the shutout became something of a news item. Thus "Chicago" became synonymous with shutout. The second, and more likely, theory: Chicago's National League team of 1876 won eight games by shutout, all hurled by its sole pitcher, the legendary Al Spalding. In those days, eight shutouts in a season was a remarkable feat, and so "Chicago" came to mean a blanking. (It seems that it would have been more proper to call it a "Spalding," but why quibble?) Also BLANK, SHUT OUT, and WHITEWASH.

n. A shutout. Also KALSOMINE and WHITEWASH.

Chicago slide: n. A slide in which the runner swings wide of a base and hooks his foot around the base to elude a fielder who is trying to tag him out. The term is traced to Mike "King" Kelly, who made the slide famous while playing with Chicago's National League team during the 1880s. A song was even written about him: "Slide, Kelly, Slide." Also FADE-AWAY SLIDE, FALLAWAY SLIDE, and HOOK SLIDE.

Chinese home run: n. A batted ball that barely reaches the stands for a home run. A cartoonist named T.A. Dorgan is credited with coining the phrase, a reference mainly to the poorly paid Chinese laborers who helped build America's railroads in the late 1800s. Sportwriters subsequently invented synonyms for "Chinese home run," such as "homer foo young," "chow mein smash," and "egg roll bingle." One writer nicknamed New York's Polo Grounds "The Harlem Joss House" because many home runs were hit over its short fences.

chin music: n. A brushback pitch, usually a fastball that goes "singing" underneath the batter's chin. See BRUSHBACK PITCH.

chop: v. To swing down at a pitch and cause it to take a high first bounce.

chop, chopper: n. A high-bounding ground ball. Also BALTIMORE CHOP, BOUNDER, BUTCHER BOY, CHOPPER, and TOPPER.

chuck: v. To throw, particularly to pitch.

CHIN MUSIC

CHICAGO SLIDE

chucker: See PITCHER.

circuit: n. 1. The complete path around the bases. 2. A league. For example, the National League, founded in 1876, is known as the "senior circuit," while the American League, founded 15 years later, is the "junior circuit."

circuit clout: n. A home run, so named because a batter runs the complete circuit of the bases after hitting a homer.

circus catch, circus play: n. A spectacular defensive play. Allegedly coined by Chicago sportswriter Charlie Seymour in the mid-1880s, "circus catch" sometimes has a negative connotation, as when a fielder makes an easy play look difficult. Also JAWN TITUS.

clang: n. An inept fielder, one who is said to have "hard hands" or "iron hands." The ball "clangs" off his hands when he tries to field it. One of the more notorious clangs in big league history was Dick Stuart, a first baseman in the late 1950s and most of the 1960s. Stuart's nickname was "Dr. Strangeglove." Compare SOFT HANDS.

cleanup: n. The fourth position in the batting order. The man who bats fourth is counted on to "clean up" the bases; that is, to drive in any of the batters ahead of him who are on base.

cleats: See SHOES.

closed stance: n. A batting stance in which the batter's top foot (the left foot on a righthanded batter, the right foot on a lefthanded batter) is closer than the other foot to the side of the batter's box nearer home plate. Thus the batter's body is "closed" to the pitcher. Compare OPEN STANCE and PARALLEL STANCE.

closer: n. A pitcher, especially a starting pitcher, who has the stamina and the tenacity to finish most of his games.

clothesline, clothesliner: n. A line drive whose flight is as straight as a clothesline.

clubhouse lawyer: n. A player who often complains and makes excuses, especially to teammates and media representatives in the clubhouse. See ALIBI IKE, JAKE, JAKER, and PEBBLE PICKER.

coach's box: n. One of two rectangular areas, outlined in white near first base and third base, in which the first base and third base coaches stand during a game. Each box is parallel to and 8 feet from the foul line, and is 20 feet long. Both coaches are required to stay inside the boxes during play, but this rule is not stringently followed or enforced.

collar: n. A hitless performance by a batter in a game. When a batter goes 0 for 4, for example, he "wears the collar" for being figuratively tamed and leashed by the opposing pitcher. See GO OFER.
    v. To hold an opposing batter or team hitless.

College of Coaches: n. Chicago Cub owner Philip Wrigley's concept of rotating managers during the regular season. The "college" was in session in 1961 and 1962. Wrigley felt that the lowly Cubs, who had played under managers of every temperament and had not won a pennant since 1945, needed something radical to shake them up. The plan was scrapped when the owner finally heeded the players' complaints that they were getting conflicting counsel from the various skippers. For the record, the college's "faculty" consisted of Vedie Himsl, Harry Craft, Elvin Tappe, Lou Klein, Charlie Metro, and Bob Kennedy. The Cubs' combined record for those two seasons, during which they finished ninth both times, was 123 wins, 193 losses, and a .389 winning (so to speak) percentage.

comebacker: n. A ground ball that is hit directly at, and usually fielded by, the pitcher.

Commissioner of Baseball: n. The official ultimate authority in baseball, whose main duties are investigating and punishing acts that he may view as not being in "the best interests of baseball"; settling disputes between the two major leagues; and resolving labor struggles between baseball's club owners and players. The commissioner is selected and paid by the owners, a fact that detractors of the office point to as evidence of the commissioner's allegiance to the men who hire him and pay his salary. After the Black Sox Scandal of 1920 and years of confused committee leadership, the owners decided to hire a single commissioner and chose Judge Kenesaw Mountain Landis for the job. He took office on January 12, 1921, and served until his death in 1944. Landis was succeeded by Happy Chandler, who held the office until 1951. Chandler was followed by Ford Frick (1951–1965), General William D. Eckert (1965–1969), Bowie Kuhn (1969–1984), and Peter Ueberroth (1984–). See NATIONAL COMMISSION.

commit oneself: v. To make a half-swing but to swing far enough for the home plate umpire to call a strike. Also BREAK THE WRISTS, GO AROUND, and PULL THE TRIGGER. Compare CHECK SWING.

complete game: n. A game that is started and finished by the same pitcher. In doing so, he is credited with a "complete game." Also ROUTE-GOING PERFORMANCE. See GO THE DISTANCE and GO THE ROUTE.

contact hitter: n. A batter who has little to medium power but regularly gets base hits by making contact with the ball.

control pitcher: n. A pitcher who throws to exact locations around the plate. Such a hurler, said to have good or great "control," relies most often on slow breaking balls, though fastballers like Sandy Koufax and Dwight Gooden are also known as outstanding control pitchers. Also FINESSE

PITCHER and PITCHER (3.). Compare POWER PITCHER and THROWER.

cookie: n. A pitch that is easy to hit. A hitter looks at such a pitch with all the glee of a child who is about to bite into a cookie. Also FAT PITCH and LOLLIPOP. Compare CRIPPLE.

Cooperstown: n. The small, picturesque town in upstate New York where the National Baseball Hall of Fame and Museum is located. See NATIONAL BASEBALL HALL OF FAME AND MUSEUM.

cork: n. An ace relief pitcher, one who comes into a game and "puts a cork" in a rally by the opposing team. Also STOPPER.

corked bat: n. A bat that has had cork inserted into the barrel. Although corked bats are illegal, some batters sneak them into action because they are light and add distance to batted balls. Also PLUGGED BAT. See DOCTORED BAT.

count: n. The number of balls and strikes on a batter during his at bat.

country-fair hitter: n. An excellent hitter. The term refers to the big strong rural boys who played ball at country fairs. Later it became "pretty fair country hitter." Occasionally "country-fair" is used as an adjective meaning "show-offish."

cousin: n. An easy opponent. A batter who has always been successful against a particular pitcher, or vice versa, regards him as a "cousin." The word was coined during the 1920s by Waite Hoyt, who said he found as much pleasure in playing an easy opponent as he did in seeing an actual cousin. Hoyt pitched for the great New York Yankee teams of the 1920s, teams that certainly encountered many a "cousin" on the playing field.

crank: See FAN (n.).

crew chief: n. The umpire who is in charge of the crew of umpires working a particular game.

cripple: n. A pitch that the batter expects to be easy to hit because he is well ahead of the pitcher in the count; for example, a pitch with a count of three balls and one strike is usually a cripple. The word derives from the fact that a pitcher in this situation is "crippled." He has little choice (and the batter knows it) but to try to throw a pitch over the plate for a strike. In a cripple situation, the batter knows that the pitch should be hittable before it is thrown, unlike a COOKIE, FAT PITCH, or LOLLIPOP, terms that suggest pitches that appear hittable only after they have been thrown and as they approach home plate.

cripple shooter: n. A batter who is well ahead of the pitcher in the count and expecting a "cripple," an easy pitch to hit.

crossfire: n. A pitch that is thrown with a sidearm delivery and crosses the plate diagonally.

Cuban fork ball: n. A spitball. Cuban native Pedro Ramos, who pitched in the majors from 1955 to 1970, gave this euphemistic name to his spitter. Besides, Ramos reasoned, the pitch did behave something like a fork ball. See DOCTORED BALL and SPITBALL.

cue shot: n. A ball that is struck off the end of the bat, much like a shot made with a cue stick in billiards.

cup of coffee: n. A brief stay on a major league team. When a minor leaguer is called up to the majors and stays for a short period before being sent back to the minors, he is said to have stayed just long enough to have a "cup of coffee."

curtain-raiser: n. The first game of a series, a doubleheader, or a season. Also LIDLIFTER.

curve, curve ball: n. A pitch that bends in its flight toward home plate, usually down and away from the point from which it was thrown. Several pitchers claimed that they introduced the curve in the mid-1800s, but the general consensus is that Arthur "Candy" Cummings was the first pitcher to throw a curve ball, managing the feat as early as 1864. He introduced the curve to professional baseball in 1872 when he went 34 and 19 with the New York Mutuals of the National Association. That same year, an old rule prohibiting pitchers from snapping their wrists when throwing was repealed, thus officially introducing the curve to baseball. Also BENDER, BREAKING BALL, DEAD FISH, DEUCE, DIPSY-DO, DROP PITCH, FISH, FISH HOOK, HOOK, INCURVE, INSHOOT, JUG, JUG HANDLE, MACKEREL, NUMBER TWO, OUTCURVE, OUTSHOOT, PRETZEL, RAINBOW, ROUNDHOUSE, SLANT, SNAKE, UNCLE CHARLIE, YAKKER, and YELLOW HAMMER.

curveball change: See CHANGE, CHANGE OF PACE, and CHANGE-UP.

curving upshoot: See SUBMARINE (n.).

cut: v. 1. To swing at a pitch. 2. To avoid stepping on a base while advancing two or more bases. "Cutting" is an illegal, and usually deliberate, attempt by the runner to save a step or two.
    n. A batter's swing at a pitch.

cut ball: n. A ball that has been slightly slit or scraped, usually secretly by the pitcher, so as to give it an exaggerated curve when pitched. Cutting a ball is illegal. See DOCTORED BALL.

cut down: See GUN DOWN.

cutter: n. A batter, one who takes swings or "cuts."

cycle: n. A single, double, triple, and home run in one game by a batter. See HIT FOR THE CYCLE.

Cy Young Award: n. The annual award recognizing the best pitchers in the American and National Leagues. Introduced in 1956 and voted on by the Baseball Writers Association of America, the award was the invention of baseball commissioner Ford Frick, who felt that pitchers were too often ignored in the Most Valuable Player balloting because they played only every four or five days. Through 1966 only one pitcher was honored each season. But the baseball writers petitioned Frick's successor as commissioner, William Eckert, to decree that a Cy Young Award be given annually to a pitcher from each league. Eckert agreed, and the change took effect in 1967. Denton True "Cy" Young won 511 games in the major leagues from 1890 to 1911, the most by any pitcher in baseball history. He is the only hurler to have won 200 games in both the American and National Leagues.

daisy-clipper, daisy-cutter: n. A sharply hit ground ball.

Daniel Webster: n. A player who often argues with umpires. Webster was the American statesman known during the mid-1800s as "The Great Orator."

darter: See LINE DRIVE.

day for a player: n. A ceremony, usually preceding a ball game, in which a popular player, usually one who is about to retire, receives praise and prizes from his teammates, his bosses, and his fans. Special days for players were held as far back as the early 1900s. Pittsburgh Pirate shortstop Honus Wagner and Boston Red Sox pitcher Cy Young had "days" in 1908. The financial value of the gifts that an honored player received in those days pales when compared to the amazing smorgasbord of goodies bestowed on the modern honoree. Probably the most famous players' "days" were the two saddest, those held for Babe Ruth and Lou Gehrig. Both New York Yankee greats were near death when they were honored, and both gave memorable farewell speeches at Yankee Stadium. On his day in 1939, Gehrig told the crowd, "Today I consider myself the luckiest man on the face of the earth. I might have been given a bad break, but I've got an awful lot to live for." Eight years later, Ruth said during his ceremony,

"You know this baseball game of ours . . . the only real game, I think, in the world—baseball."

daylight play: n. A play in which an infielder furtively goes to a base from which a runner is leading and takes a pick-off throw from the catcher or pitcher. The term derives from the "daylight" between the runner and his base.

day-night doubleheader: n. A doubleheader in which one game is started in early afternoon and another game started in the evening. The ballpark is emptied after the first game, and a separate admission is charged for each game. See DOUBLEHEADER.

dead ball: n. 1. A ball that is not in play. Among the numerous occasions when a ball is called "dead" are when a foul ball is not caught by a fielder, a batter is hit by a pitch, a pitcher balks, a fan touches a ball that is in play, and a batted ball hits a baserunner. 2. The heavy, slow-moving ball used in the American League before 1920, in the National League before 1921, the seasons when a more lively ball was introduced to major league play. Thus the years prior to 1920–21 are sometimes called "the dead ball era." From 1911 through 1920–21, a ball with a cork center was used and proved more lively than any ball used previously. Nonetheless, even this cork-centered ball seemed "dead" compared to the "rabbit ball" introduced in 1921. See RABBIT BALL.

dead fish: n. A curve ball, so named because its flight resembles a fish in deathly repose.

dead red: n. A fastball, or many fastballs. The name suggests the destructive "heat" of a good fastball.

deep depth: n. An expression coined by Earl Weaver, long-time manager of the Baltimore Orioles, meaning many talented reserve players. Though a redundancy, Weaver's phrase always got the point across.

delayed double-steal: n. A play in which two baserunners steal bases, with one man running on the pitch and the other man waiting to run until a play is made on the first runner. Compare DOUBLE STEAL.

delayed steal: n. A play in which a baserunner steals a base, running not on the pitch but after the catcher has returned the ball to the pitcher or during a play on another baserunner.

designated hitter: n. A player who bats for a weak-hitting teammate (usually the pitcher) in the starting lineup during the length of a game, but does not play a defensive position. The player for whom the designated hitter bats does not have to leave the game. Abbreviated DH. The American League is the only major league to use the DH rule, which was adopted before the 1973 season. Eight of the league's twelve clubs had lost money and nine failed to draw more than a million fans in 1972, thus prompting the AL owners to try the DH experiment for three years. After the trial period, the rule became permanent, although the National League has yet to adopt it. Ironically, the junior circuit vetoed the DH rule when it was proposed in 1928 by National League president John Heydler and managers John McGraw of the New York Giants and Wilbert Robinson of the Brooklyn Dodgers. The New York Yankees' Ron Blomberg was the first DH, and in his initial at bat he drew a bases-loaded walk from Boston's Luis Tiant.

designated runner: n. A player whose sole purpose is to pinch-run. There has been only one designated runner in baseball, Herb Washington, a former track star who was hired by Oakland A's owner Charlie Finley in the mid-1970s. In 109 games, including 5 in the postseason, Washington scored 33 runs and stole 30 bases, though he never batted or played a defensive position.

deuce: n. A curve ball, so called because a catcher wags two fingers when signaling for the pitcher to throw a curve.

DH: Abbreviation for DESIGNATED HITTER and DOUBLE-HEADER.

dial 8: v. To hit a home run. The term derives from the fact that in hotels, places with which professional ballplayers are familiar, one dials "8" on the telephone to get long distance. Hitting a home run is, after all, sending a ball a long distance.

diamond: n. The infield portion of a baseball field—specifically, the pattern formed by the four bases. Because it has four sides of equal length (90 feet) and four right angles, a baseball diamond is actually a tilted square. Alexander Cartwright, the true father of baseball and the head of the first organized ball team (the New York Knickerbockers), is credited with inventing the diamond design in 1845.

diamond field: n. The infield. The term originated in the late 1800s.

Dick Smith: n. A loner, a player who keeps to himself, so called for the nondescript quality of the name.

die: v. 1. To be left on base. 2. Refers to a batted ball that abruptly slows down because of high grass, wet grass, or strong wind.

dinger: n. A home run. The term is of uncertain origin.

dipsy-do: n. A curve ball, a pitch that reaches the peak of its arc and them "dips."

dirter: n. A ground ball, in the parlance of veteran player and manager Casey Stengel.

dish: n. Home plate, so named for its resemblance to a dish.

division: n. 1. One of the two leagues within each major league. Both the American and National Leagues include

Eastern and Western Divisions, more familiarly known as the East and the West. The Divisional format was adopted before the 1969 season as part of each major league's expansion from ten to twelve teams. 2. A term used before 1969 to describe half of each major league. The better teams in a league comprised the "first division," while the worse teams wallowed in the "second division."

do a Casey: v. To strike out, especially in a crucial situation, like the protagonist of the poem "Casey at the Bat." Also PULL A CASEY. See "CASEY AT THE BAT."

doctor: n. A pitcher who puts an illegal substance or blemish on a ball before throwing it.
     v. To tamper illegally with a bat, ball, or field to gain an advantage over the opponent.

doctored ball: n. A ball that has been illegally blemished or dabbed with an illegal substance, usually by a pitcher, to make the ball break sharply when thrown. Pitchers are not the only ones known for doing a little doctoring. When they were managing in the majors, Ty Cobb and Connie Mack doctored balls by freezing a batch of them whenever a slugging team was coming to town. The frozen balls would not travel so far when struck, thus stealing an advantage from a hard-hitting club. See ALTERNATIVE PITCH, CUBAN FORK BALL, CUT BALL, EMERY BALL, GREASEBALL, JELLY BALL, LOAD, LOAD UP, MARKED BALL, MUD BALL, PINE-TAR BALL, POWDER-PUFF BALL, PUFF BALL, RESIN BALL, SANDPAPER BALL, SCUFFBALL, SCUFFER, SHINE BALL, SPITBALL, and STATEN ISLAND SINKER.

doctored bat: n. A bat that has been illegally tampered with to make it lighter and more powerful. A common method of doctoring a bat is drilling a small hole at the top of the head and leaving it hollow or filling it with cork. As a result, the bat is lighter while the cork in the mass of the bat supplies extra power. See CORKED BAT, HOLLOW BAT, and PLUGGED BAT.

doctored field: n. A field that has been tended in such a way that gives an advantage to the home team. For instance, a team that likes to bunt will have its groundskeeper raise the dirt around the foul lines, which would prevent a bunted ball from rolling into foul territory. Or a team that has pitchers who give up a lot of ground balls will make sure the infield grass is kept high, so that grounders will slow down and be easily stopped by the fielders. When he was managing the Philadelphia Athletics in the early 1900s, Connie Mack ordered his grounds crew to raise the pitcher's mound in order to give his crack pitching corps an extra advantage.

Dr. Longball: n. A home run, a term coined by Baltimore Oriole manager Earl Weaver. When the Orioles went long spells without hitting a homer, Weaver would say it was time to "put in a call to Dr. Longball."

dome dong: n. A home run hit inside a dome stadium. The term derives from home runs hit inside Seattle's Kingdome, where homers are ridiculously frequent.

donkey: n. A rookie, so called because he sometimes makes an ass of himself.

double: n. A batted ball that allows the batter to reach second base safely without an error by the defense. Also TWO-BAGGER and TWO-BASE HIT.

Doubleday, Abner: n. The man who for years was incorrectly credited with being the father of modern baseball. Doubleday, the legend went, invented the game in Cooperstown, New York, in 1839. In fact, Doubleday was a West Point plebe in 1839, and probably was too busy to invent the national pastime. In 1905 a special baseball commission—composed of four baseball officials and two United States senators—named

Doubleday as the game's inventor in an earnest though cock-eyed attempt to trace some origin of the new national pastime. Later studies showed that Alexander Cartwright, not Abner Doubleday, was the true father of the national pastime, although the Doubleday fiction seems nearly as popular as ever among the general baseball public. See CARTWRIGHT, ALEXANDER.

doubleheader: n. Two games played consecutively at the same site. Abbreviated DH. The term comes from railroad parlance, in which a "doubleheader" refers to a train with two engines. The first doubleheader in major league history took place on September 25, 1882, between the Worcester and Providence teams of the National League. Each team won a game. Also TWIN BILL. See DAY-NIGHT DOUBLE-HEADER and TWI-NIGHT DOUBLEHEADER.

double play: n. A defensive play in which two outs are made. A double play can be made in numerous ways, including fielding a ground ball, forcing a baserunner at one base and then relaying the ball so as to force at another base; striking out the batter and then throwing out a baserunner who is attempting to steal; and catching a batted ball in the air and relaying to a base which a runner has left without tagging up. Also PITCHER'S BEST FRIEND and TWIN KILLING.

double steal: n. A play in which two baserunners simultaneously try to steal a base. Compare DELAYED DOUBLE STEAL.

double up: v. To get the second out in a double play.

doughnut: n. A metal doughnut-shaped weight that a player places around the head of his bat while taking warm-up swings in the on-deck circle. Elston Howard, a catcher for the New York Yankees, is credited with introducing the doughnut to the majors around 1960.

down: Out, as in "With that second strike out, there are now two down in the inning."

downtown: n. The area beyond the outfield wall, specifically, where a home run lands. When a player hits a homer, he "goes downtown."

downtowner: n. A home run. See DOWNTOWN.

dribbler: n. A ground ball that travels slowly and takes many bounces.

drooler: n. A spitball. The nickname should be self-explanatory.

drop off the table: This expression refers to an overhand breaking pitch that ends with such a sudden and severe curve that it appears, from the batter's view, as if the ball had dropped off a table.

drop pitch: n. A curve ball that breaks down toward the plate.

ducks on the pond: n. Runners on base, especially in a bases loaded situation, whom the batter is expected to drive in, just as a hunter is expected to bag "ducks on the pond." The expression is credited to Arch McDonald, a former radio broadcaster for the Washington Senators and the New York Yankees.

dugout: n. A long enclosed area in which a team's players, coaches, manager, and other personnel sit during a game. Usually sunken a few feet into the ground, each dugout is in foul territory and faces one of the foul lines. Dugouts became common with the erection of the modern steel-and-concrete baseball stadiums in the early 1900s.

dust, dust off a batter: See BRUSH BACK.

duster: See BRUSHBACK PITCH.

dying quail: n. A weakly hit fly ball that falls toward the area behind the infield. Named for the way it falls heavily to the ground, like a bird that's been shot, a "dying quail" often drops between the infielders and the outfielders for a base hit. Also BLOOP, BLOOPER, FLARE, LOOPER, QUAIL, QUAIL SHOT, TEXAS LEAGUER, and WOUNDED DUCK. Compare PARACHUTE.

early bloomer: n. A player who performs well early in a season or in his career but then fails to maintain the same level of achievement. Also MORNING GLORY. Compare PHENOM.

earned run: n. A run that scores without virtue of an error by the defense and is included when figuring a pitcher's earned run average. See EARNED RUN AVERAGE. Compare UNEARNED RUN.

earned run average: n. The statistic measuring the number of earned runs that a pitcher allows every nine innings. To figure earned run average (abbreviated ERA), multiply the number of a pitcher's earned runs by nine and then divide that total by the number of his innings pitched. Baseball writers and officials started computing earned run average in the 1860s, and then suddenly stopped in the 1880s, only to resume officially for good in 1912 in the National League and a year later in the American League.

easy out: n. A weak batter, one who is especially easy to get out. Also OUT MAN. Compare TOUGH OUT.

eject: v. As umpire, to dismiss anyone at a ball game, from a member of either team to a spectator, from the premises for the duration of the game. Also RUN, THUMB, THROW OUT, TOSS, and TOSS OUT.

ejection: n. An umpire's dismissal of anyone at a ball game, from a team member to a spectator, from the premises for the duration of the game. Also HEAVE-HO.

Elysian Fields: n. The site in Hoboken, New Jersey, where the first game with modern baseball rules was played on June 19, 1846. In that game the New York Nine defeated Alexander Cartwright's Knickerbockers 23–1. See CARTWRIGHT, ALEXANDER.

emery ball: n. A ball that has been scratched on one side—with an emery cloth, emery powder, sandpaper, etc.—to cause it to curve sharply when pitched. The emery ball, like other doctored pitches, was outlawed by the major leagues in 1920. Since then, only one pitcher has been ejected from a game, suspended, and fined for throwing a "scuffball," as it is known. Rick Honeycutt, while pitching for the Seattle Mariners in 1980, was caught with a poorly concealed thumbtack on his glove hand, which he was using to scuff the ball. Also SCUFFBALL and SCUFFER. See DOCTORED BALL.

English: n. The spin on a ball. The word is said to derive from either the familiar expression "body English" or the once-prevalent American view that the English were not above using trickery and deception to win their way.

ephus pitch: n. A slow high-arcing pitch intended to make the batter pop up. "Ephus" (sometimes spelled "eephus") was the name of Pittsburgh Pirate pitcher Truett "Rip" Sewell's blooper pitch. His teammate Maurice Van Robays coined the word, explaining to reporters that it was a "nothin' pitch, and eephus ain't nothin'." Sewell began using the high-arcing pitch in 1941 and had a fairly successful career with it, winning 42 games in 1943 and 1944. Sewell and his ephus received their roughest treatment in the 1946 All-Star game, when Boston Red Sox star Ted Williams hit the only home run ever off the pitch. Close relatives are the BAL-

LOON PITCH, the BLOOPER PITCH, the BUTTERFLY, and the LALOB.

excuse-me hit: n. A blooped or grounded base hit that results when the batter tries to stop a swing but inadvertently hits the ball. The batter is almost expected to say "excuse me" for such a flimsy hit.

expansion: n. The addition of new franchises to the major leagues. From 1901 to 1960, both the American and National Leagues comprised eight teams each. The first expansion of the majors occurred in 1961 when the American League added two teams, the Los Angeles (later California) Angels and the Washington Senators. (This was a new Senator team; the old Senators left Washington at the end of 1960 and opened the 1961 season as the Minnesota Twins.) The National League expanded with the New York Mets and the Houston Colt .45s (later Astros) in 1962. Seven years later each league grew to 12 teams and went to the Divisional format, as the Kansas City Royals and Seattle Pilots (who became the Milwaukee Brewers in 1970) joined the American League and the Montreal Expos and San Diego Padres joined the senior circuit. The American League expanded again in 1977, adding the Toronto Blue Jays and the Seattle Mariners.

exploding scoreboard: n. A stadium scoreboard above which fireworks are exploded after a home run or victory by the home team. Bill Veeck, while owner of the Chicago White Sox, introduced the exploding scoreboard in 1959. It proved a hit with Chisox fans at Comiskey Park, but not always with opposing players. During one fireworks display, Cleveland Indian outfielder Jimmy Piersall angrily hurled a baseball at the scoreboard, and on another occasion, members of the New York Yankees brought sparklers with them during a series at Comiskey Park and lit them in the dugout after a Mickey Mantle home run.

extra innings: n. Innings played if a game is tied after nine full innings. If the visiting team breaks the tie in extra innings, then it must retire the home team in the bottom of the inning and still hold the lead to win the game. If the home team breaks the tie in extra innings, then the game is immediately over.

face mask: See CATCHER'S MASK.

fadeaway: n. The name of the screwball thrown by Christy Mathewson, the legendary New York Giants pitcher of the early 1900s. Christy's fadeaway is considered the first screwball, though some claim he was taught the pitch by Rube Foster, the Giants' pitching coach and a control pitcher from the early days of all-Negro baseball leagues. See SCREWBALL.

fadeaway slide, fallaway slide: See CHICAGO SLIDE.

Fall Classic: See WORLD SERIES.

fan: n. A regular supporter of a particular sport, especially of one team in that sport. "Fan" reportedly was coined in the 1880s by sportswriter Sam Crane after he had overheard Chris Von der Ahe, owner of the St. Louis Browns of the American Association, describe one Browns follower as "a regular FANatic" (with the accent on the first syllable). Also ANT, BUG, CRANK, KRANK, and ROOTER.
    v. 1. To strike out by swinging at and missing a pitch, after already having two strikes. 2. To swing at and miss any pitch. 3. To strike out a batter. See STRIKE OUT.

fan's interference, fan's obstruction: n. Interference, by a fan, with a ball that is in play. If a fan sitting near the outfield foul line touches a ball that is in play, then the batter is awarded a ground-rule double. If a fan sitting near the field reaches into the playing area and prevents a fielder from making a catch, then the catch is awarded to the fielder and the batter is called out. The fan is usually booed.

far corner: n. Third base.

farm: n. A minor league, specifically one team's minor league system. A "farm club" or "farm team" is one of the teams in a major league organization's minor league chain. See MINOR LEAGUE.

farm out: v. To assign a player to a minor league team or send him "down to the farm."

fastball: n. A pitch thrown with great velocity. A major league fastball generally travels about 85 miles per hour or faster. Also ASPIRIN, ASPIRIN TABLET, BLAZER, CHEESE, DEAD RED, FOG, GAS, HEAT, HEATER, HUMMER, MUSTARD, NUMBER ONE, PEPPER, PILL, PNEUMONIA BALL, RADIO BALL, RISING FASTBALL, SEED, SMOKE, SPEEDBALL, STEAM, TAILING FASTBALL, and UPSHOOT.

fat part of the bat: n. The barrel, or heavy end, of the bat. Also HEAD OF THE BAT and MEAT OF THE BAT.

fat pitch: n. A pitch that seems so easy to hit that the ball looks "fat" to the batter. Also COOKIE and LOLLIPOP. Compare CRIPPLE.

Federal League: n. A baseball major league that existed in 1914 and 1915. Previously a minor league, the Federal League in 1914 declared itself a competitor of the two existing major leagues, the American and the National, and even lured the other leagues' players with its large supply of funds. But prior to the 1916 season, after two years of costly court battles, the three leagues came to a peaceful settlement of the situation: The National and American Leagues assumed responsibility for $385,000 in Fed player contracts, allowed two Fed owners to purchase teams in the other leagues and paid off the debts of other Federal League investors. Fed franchises were located in Chicago, St. Louis, Pittsburgh, Kansas City, Newark, Baltimore, Buffalo, Brooklyn, and Indianapolis. The teams played only among themselves, not against American or National League clubs.

field general: n. A manager of a baseball team, sometimes also called the "field manager." See MANAGER.

field umpire: n. An umpire stationed at first base, second base, or third base—that is, any umpire who is not the home plate umpire.

fielding average, fielding percentage: n. A statistic that reflects a player's defensive ability. To figure fielding percentage, divide the total number of a player's assists and put-outs by the total number of his chances. If he has 485 assists and put-outs in 500 chances, then his fielding percentage is .970.

fielding glove: n. The large leather mitt, with a webbed pocket to facilitate catching the ball, worn by defensive players. Charles White, a first baseman for Boston's National Association club in 1875, reportedly was the first player to wear a glove. His flimsy unpadded glove was jeered at but later imitated by his opponents. However, the fielding glove did not become a common piece of equipment until the 1880s. Through the 1920s, most gloves were little more than flat pieces of leather with no pocket, also known as "pancake" gloves. Nowadays gloves are so large that players often have trouble digging the ball out of the pocket once they have made a grab. Until the early 1950s, players left their gloves on the field before going in to bat. Baseball officials ended the custom for fear that the gloves could affect play or cause injury, though such incidents were surprisingly infrequent. See CATCHER'S MITT.

finesse pitcher: n. A pitcher who relies on his control of his breaking pitches to get batters out. He works with "finesse," unlike the power pitcher, who tries to retire batters with one fastball after another. Also CONTROL PITCHER and PITCHER (3). Compare POWER PITCHER and THROWER.

fingernail ball: n. A knuckle ball, so named because the pitcher grips the ball with his fingernails. Still, the pitch is almost exclusively known as a "knuckle ball," even though few pitchers have ever used their knuckles to grip the ball.

fireman: n. A relief pitcher, one who is expected to come into a game and stop a rally by the other team, or "put out the fire." The name was first applied to Johnny Murphy, a relief pitcher for the New York Yankees during the 1930s and 1940s. In fact, he was nicknamed "Fireman." Also ICE MAN.

first, first base: n. 1. The base 90 feet from home plate, on the right field foul line. This is the base to which the batter runs after hitting the ball. Also GATEWAY. 2. The position played by the first baseman. 3. A nickname for the first baseman.

first baseman: n. The defensive player who positions himself near first base. His main responsibility is, while keeping a foot on first base, to take throws from other defensive players who have fielded ground balls and are throwing to first base to put out the batter. Also FIRST and FIRST BASE.

first-base coach: n. A coach for the batting team who stands in the coach's box in foul territory near first base.

fish, fish hook: n. A curve ball.

fist: v. To hit a ball off the handle of the bat, where the batter positions his fists.

flag: See PENNANT.

flap: See GOAT'S BEARD.

flare: n. A looping fly ball toward an area between an infielder and an outfielder. "Flare," which came into use in the mid-1970s, is a modern synonym for "Texas leaguer."
    v. To hit a flare.

flip glasses: See PULL-DOWN SUNGLASSES.

flipper: n. 1. A pitcher. 2. A fielder's throwing arm, particularly a pitcher's arm.

floater: See KNUCKLE BALL.

flutterball: See KNUCKLE BALL.

fog: n. A fastball or many fastballs.
    v. To throw a fastball or fastballs, or "fog it by 'em."

foot in the bucket: n. A batting position in which the batter lifts his front foot and steps in the direction of the nearer baseline. (A right-handed batter steps toward third base, a left-handed batter toward first.) The phrase comes from the days when water buckets were kept in dugouts. A batter with such an open batting stance was said to be, in somewhat exaggerated terms, putting his "foot in the bucket" or "stepping in the bucket." Al Simmons, a major league outfielder from 1924 to 1944, had his foot in the bucket so often that he was nicknamed "Bucketfoot Al."

fork ball: n. A pitch that curves down and has relatively little spin. The name derives from the grip pitchers use to throw the pitch—index and middle fingers spread wide atop the ball. The fork ball came into general use after 1920, when the spitball and other doctored pitches were banned.

foshball: n. The name for the type of fork ball thrown by Baltimore Oriole pitcher Mike Boddicker, who came up with the pitch during the 1983 season. Boddicker's teammates described it as a cross between a fork ball and a dead fish—thus, foshball.

FOOT IN THE BUCKET

foul pole: n. One of the two poles that mark where each foul line intersects with the outfield fence. Any batted ball that lands between these poles is fair. Any batted ball that hits a foul pole is a home run. Also POLE.

four-bagger, four-master, four-ply poke, four-ply wallop: n. A home run.

frame: n. An inning.

franchise: n. 1. A baseball club and its entire organization. 2. A player who is clearly the most valuable member of his team. This term is used in other sports as well as in baseball.

free pass: n. A base on balls.

free swinger: n. A batter who tends to swing often and at all types of pitches.

free ticket, free trip: n. A base on balls.

freeze the batter: v. To throw a pitch that makes the batter "freeze" in his stance. Usually this results when the batter receives a pitch that he wasn't expecting.

freeze the runner: v. To cause a baserunner to "freeze" in his lead. A pitcher, once he has reached the set position, can freeze a runner simply by looking at him.

French baseball terms: French-speaking people have been watching and playing baseball since as early as 1870, when pickup games were held in Montreal's Atwater Park. Montreal had the first professional baseball team in a French-speaking country with the establishment of the Montreal Royals in the Eastern League in 1897, and later the first major league ball team with the founding of the National League Montreal Expos in 1967. Ten years later, the Toronto Blue Jays joined the American League. As Canadian baseball has emerged, so has a French vocabulary of baseball terms, some of which are listed below (see also SPANISH BASEBALL TERMS):

ballpark = "terrain de jeu"

bleachers = "estrades à prix populaire"

bullpen = "enclos d'exercise des releveurs"

doubleheader = "programme double"

extra innings = "prolongation"

frozen rope = "coup en flèche"

going, going, gone! = "Et elle est partie!"

home run = "coup de circuit"

knuckle ball = "balle papillon"

live arm = "bras puissant"

Most Valuable Player = "le joueur le plus utile à son équipe"

pinch hitter = "frapper auxiliaire"

play ball! = "Au jeu!"

shoestring catch = "vol au sol"

Texas leaguer = "ballon à l'entre-champs"

triple = "triple"

frozen rope: n. A straight and sharply hit line drive. Also ROPE.

fungo: n. 1. A fielding drill, usually conducted before a game, in which a coach or player tosses a ball into the air and, with a fungo bat, hits fly balls and ground balls to fielders. 2. A fly ball or ground ball hit with a fungo bat. The practice of fungo-hitting began in the 1860s, although the origin of the word is uncertain. Some historians claim it derives from "fungus," a reference to the soft wood used to make fungo bats. Others say "fungo" comes from an old Scottish verb, "fung," meaning "to toss." Another possible root is the word "fungible," a thing that is substituted for something else, just as a fungo bat replaces a conventional bat during a fungo drill. Still others believe that the word has its derivation in a rhyme recited during early versions of fungo, a rhyme consisting of the words "run and go."

fungo bat: n. A bat with a long thin handle and a thick head, used during a fungo drill.

fungo circle: n. A circle measuring about five to ten feet in diameter, in which a coach or player stands while hitting balls during a fungo drill. Most ball fields have two fungo circles in foul territory near home plate, one alongside either baseline.

gamer: n. 1. A tenacious player, particularly one who plays while injured. 2. See GAME-WINNER.

game-winner, game-winning hit: n. The hit that drives in the game-winning run. Also GAMER.

game-winning run batted in: n. The run batted in that gives a team a lead it never loses. Abbreviated GWRBI. Both major leagues began officially keeping count of this statistic in 1980.

gap: n. The area between two outfielders. Also ALLEY and POWER ALLEY.

gapper, gap shot: n. A ball hit into one of the gaps in the outfield. Also TWEENER.

garden: n. The outfield. Also ORCHARD and PASTURE.

gardener: n. An outfielder, because he romps around the outfield, also known as the "garden."

gas: n. A fastball or many fastballs.
v. To throw a fastball or fastballs, as in "Gas it by 'em."

Gashouse Gang: n. A nickname for the feisty, hard-playing St. Louis Cardinal teams of the mid-1930s. With such players as Leo "The Lip" Durocher, Dizzy Dean, Paul "Daffy" Dean, John "Pepper" Martin, Frankie Frisch, and Joe "Ducky" Medwick, the Gashouse Gang won the 1934 World Series. Various sportswriters—including Tom Meany, Frank Graham, and Gerry Schumacher—have been credited with coining the nickname. Whoever the author was, his intention was to associate the rough-and-tumble Cards with the seedy Gashouse district of New York City.

gateway: n. First base, so called because it is the first stop in a complete path around the bases.

get all of it (the pitch): v. To hit a ball solidly and for a long distance.

get a piece of the ball: v. To swing at a pitch and make slight contact with the ball.

get around on a fastball: v. To swing the bat quickly enough to make good contact with a fastball.

get good wood on the ball: v. To hit a ball solidly.

get under the ball: v. To swing upward at a pitch and cause the ball to fly in a high arc.

Gillette: n. A pitch thrown close to the batter's head. Such a pitch, thrown by a hurler with a reputation as a "headhunter" or "barber," is said to give the batter a "close shave" (like the razor blade manufactured by the Gillette company, for which the pitch is named). See BRUSHBACK PITCH.

glove: See BATTING GLOVE and FIELDING GLOVE.

glove man: n. A player who has a reputation as an excellent fielder. Also LEATHERMAN.

go around: v. To take a half-swing that moves just far enough around for the home plate umpire to call a strike. Also BREAK

THE WRISTS, COMMIT ONESELF, and PULL THE TRIG-GER. Compare CHECK SWING.

goat's beard: n. A plastic or leather flap that hangs down from a catcher's mask and is intended to shield the catcher's throat from foul tips or flying bats. About 1890 baseball player and entrepreneur A.G. Spalding marketed a catcher's mask that included a neck-protecting extension made of a dogskin covering and goat hair filling. In the mid-1970s, Los Angeles Dodger trainer Bill Buhler devised the modern goat's beard after a serious neck injury to Dodger catcher Steve Yeager. By now most catchers and home plate umpires wear goat's beards on their face masks. Also FLAP.

go deep: v. To hit a home run.

go down on strikes: v. To strike out.

go down looking: v. To strike out by failing to swing at a pitch that the home plate umpire calls the third strike.

go down swinging: v. To strike out by swinging at and missing a pitch, after already having two strikes.

go downtown: v. To hit a home run.

"Going, going, gone!": n. A standard phrase used by baseball broadcasters when announcing a home run. Coined in 1929 by Cincinnati Reds announcer Harry Hartman, the expression was later popularized by New York Yankee broadcaster Mel Allen.

Gold Glove Award: n. An award presented annually to the oustanding defensive players of both major leagues. The award was created by the Rawlings Sporting Goods Company and *The Sporting News* in 1957. That first year, the Gold Glove team comprised the best fielders from both the American and National Leagues, so only nine trophies were handed out. Thereafter, a full Gold Glove team was selected from each league.

gonfalon: See PENNANT.

good field, no hit: adj. An expression referring to a player who is a good fielder but a poor hitter. Havana native Mike Gonzalez, a National League player from 1912 to 1932 and later a major league scout, is credited with inventing the phrase. After scouting a young prospect, Gonzalez wired back to the team that was interested in the player, "Good field, no hit." Gonzalez's English may have been a bit broken, but his message was clear.

go on the pitch: v. To begin running toward the next base just before the pitcher delivers the ball toward home plate.

goose egg: n. A zero, particularly a zero on a stadium scoreboard, as when a team fails to score during an inning or several consecutive innings. The term has its root in the cricket term "achieve a duck's egg," which referred to a batsman who had failed to score. During baseball's early years, the phrase was Americanized to "goose egg."

gopher ball, gopher pitch: n. A pitch that the batter hits for a home run. Though of uncertain origin, the expression may have come from Lefty Gomez, the masterful and witty New York Yankee pitcher of the 1930s and 1940s. According to one story, Gomez told a Wisconsin radio interviewer that a gopher ball is "an errant pitch that will sometimes gopher a double, sometimes gopher a triple, and too often gopher a home run."

go the distance: v. To pitch a complete game. Also GO THE ROUTE. See COMPLETE GAME and ROUTE-GOING PERFORMANCE.

go the other way: v. To hit a ball to the opposite field.

go the route: See GO THE DISTANCE.

go with the pitch: v. To hit to the opposite field a pitch that is outside of the strike zone and away from the batter.

grand slam: n. A home run with the bases loaded. The term is said to derive from the game of contract bridge, in which a "grand slam" is the taking of all 13 tricks. The first recorded grand slam was hit on September 10, 1881, by Roger Connor, a first baseman for the Troy Trojans of the National League. Connor's slam, which help beat Worcester 8–7, was one of his two home runs that season. Lou Gehrig of the New York Yankees hit 23 grand slams during his career, still a major league record. Baseball was the first sport to use the expression, although golf and tennis began using "grand slam" in the 1930s and 1940s in referring to an athlete who had won four major tournaments in one year.

Grapefruit League: n. The unofficial name for the group of major league teams that encamp in Florida for spring training. Compare CACTUS LEAGUE. See SPRING TRAINING.

grassburner, grass clipper, grass cutter: n. A sharply hit ground ball.

gravy hop: n. A ground ball that takes a high and easy-to-field bounce toward a defensive player. Also BIG BILL and CHARITY HOP.

greaseball: n. A pitch that has been illegally dabbed with a substance such as hair cream, to make it break sharply when thrown. See DOCTORED BALL.

green fly: n. A baseball groupie, especially a woman who, with the pestering persistence of a fly, follows ballplayers while they're away from the ballpark. The term may also apply to anyone who is a nuisance to a ballplayer, such as a writer. See BASEBALL ANNIE.

GREEN FLY

green light: n. A signal, relayed from the manager via a base coach (usually the third-base coach), for a batter to swing at the next pitch, or for a baserunner to try to steal or continue rounding the bases.

groove: v. To throw a pitch directly over the middle of the plate. When a pitcher throws such a ball, he is said to have "grooved a pitch" to the batter.

n. 1. The center of the strike zone. A pitch thrown here is "right in the groove." 2. A successful streak for an individual player or for a team, as in "With ten hits in his last four games, he's in a groove." 3. During the early 1900s, a "groove" was a player's weakest point; for example, a batter's inability to hit a curve ball, a pitcher's lack of a good fastball.

ground ball, grounder: n. A batted ball that bounces at least once on the ground. Also BALTIMORE CHOP, BOUNCER, BOUNDER, BUTCHER BOY, CHOP, CHOPPER, DAISY-CLIP-PER, DAISY-CUTTER, DRIBBLER, GRASSBURNER, GRASS-CLIPPER, GRASS-CUTTER, HOPPER, LAWN MOWER, NUB-BER, ROLLER, SQUIBBER, TAPPER, WORMBURNER, and WORMKILLER.

guardian angel: See ANGEL.

guard the line: v. To position oneself close to either the left or right foul line. This term usually pertains to a first baseman or third baseman who, late in a close game, will play close to the foul line to prevent a ball from being hit down the line for extra bases. Also PROTECT THE LINE.

guard the plate: v. To prevent a called third strike by swinging at (and, it is the batter's hope, hitting) a pitch that looks close enough to the strike zone for the home plate umpire to rule the pitch the third strike. Also PROTECT THE PLATE.

gun: v. To throw with great velocity.

n. A strong throwing arm. Also BAZOOKA, CANNON and RIFLE.

gun down: v. To put out a baserunner by making a strong throw. Also CUT DOWN.

gun shy: adj. Afraid of the ball. This term is generally used to describe a batter who fears being hit by a pitched ball.

half swing: See CHECK SWING.

Hall of Fame: See NATIONAL BASEBALL HALL OF FAME AND MUSEUM.

ham-and-egg reliever: n. A relief pitcher whose primary role is to come into games that are already virtually decided. He is reliable but nondescript, like a meal of ham and eggs. Also MOP-UP MAN.

hamburger league: n. A minor league, so called because the players can afford only hamburgers for dinner, as opposed to the pricey steaks on which major leaguers dine.

hand: n. An at bat. Until the 1870s, an at bat was known as a "hand," a term that men's baseball clubs of the day adapted from card games.

handcuff: v. To give difficulty to an opponent. A pitcher "handcuffs" an opposing team by allowing them few hits. A ground ball "handcuffs" a fielder when it takes a bounce that is difficult to play.

handle hit: n. A base hit that was struck off the handle of the bat.

hang a curve ball: v. To throw a curve ball that breaks high in the strike zone. Batters usually hit "hanging curves" great distances.

hard hands: See IRON HANDS.

hassock: n. A base.

HBP: Abbreviation for HIT BY THE PITCH.

headhunter: See BARBER.

head of the bat: See FAT PART OF THE BAT.

heat: n. A fastball or many fastballs.

heater: n. A fastball.

heave-ho: See EJECTION.

heaver: n. A pitcher.

heavy ball: n. A pitch or batted ball that has a great deal of spin. Thus, the ball feels heavy to the player who catches it. Compare LIGHT BALL.

hesitation pitch: n. A pitch thrown after the pitcher has hesitated in his wind-up. Satchel Paige was the most famous practitioner of the hesitation pitch, which can be delivered at various speeds.

hickory: n. A bat, so called because bats were once made from this type of wood.

hidden ball trick: n. A trick play in which a baserunner is tagged out by a fielder who has been hiding the ball in his glove. For example, the first baseman will pretend to hand the ball to the pitcher but will actually keep it in his own glove. He will return to his position to guard the runner at first base, and after the runner has taken a lead, the first baseman will reach over and tag him, thus producing an out and humiliation for the unfortunate runner.

high hard one: n. A fastball thrown high in or above the strike zone.

high sky: n. A cloudless sky. Because there are no clouds blocking the sun, a high sky often creates problems for fielders trying to catch fly balls.

hill: See PITCHER'S MOUND.

hit and run: n. A prearranged offensive play in which a runner on first base starts toward second base as the pitcher releases the ball to home plate, making the batter obligated to try to hit the ball so as to allow the runner to advance. Ideally, the batter will hit the ball to a spot in the field vacated by a defensive player, either the second baseman or the shortstop, who has gone to cover second base with the intention of taking a throw from the catcher and tagging out the runner. Or, the batter could hit the ball at an infielder who, because of the runner's jump, has no option but to retire the batter at first base; thus, the runner has been advanced. If the batter swings at and misses the ball, the runner must slide into second in an attempt to steal the base. Compare with RUN AND HIT, a play in which the batter is not under any obligation to swing at the pitch.
    v. To do a hit and run.

hit behind the runner: v. To hit a ball to the right side of the field, behind the baserunner who is moving from first base.

hit by the pitch: Struck by a pitched ball while batting. Abbreviated HBP. Batters who were hit by the pitch were not awarded first base until 1884 in the American Association and 1887 in the National League. See TAKE ONE FOR THE TEAM.

hitch in the swing: n. A dropping of the hands, or a "hitch," just before a swing.

"Hit 'em where they ain't": In 1897 a reporter asked Wee Willie Keeler of the Baltimore Orioles how a man of his slight size (5 feet, 4 inches, 140 pounds) could hit for such a high average. "Simple," said Keeler. "I keep my eyes clear and I hit 'em where they ain't."

hit for the cycle: v. To achieve a cycle—a single, a double, a triple, and a home run by one batter in a game.

hitter: See BATTER.

hold: n. A statistical credit for a relief pitcher who enters a game with his team leading and eventually leaves the game with his team still in front. Although this stat awaits official adoption by baseball, most clubs have kept track of their relief pitchers' holds since about 1980. Compare SAVE and SQUANDER.

hold the runner: v. To stand close to a base and the runner occupying the base, while anticipating a pick-off throw from the pitcher. The phrase almost always applies to first basemen who "hold" runners at first.

hollow bat: n. A bat that has been slightly hollowed inside its head to make it lighter while keeping most of its mass intact. Hollow bats are illegal. See DOCTORED BAT.

home, home base, home plate: n. A flat, five-sided piece of white rubber at which the hitter stands while batting and which a runner must touch to score a run. Home plate—17 inches wide on the top edge that faces the pitcher, 8½ inches long on either perpendicular side, and 8½ inches long on the sides that slant down to a point that touches the intersection of the two foul lines—is placed opposite second base in the configuration of the diamond. Home plate forms the width of the strike zone, while the area between the batter's knees and chest constitutes the zone's length. Baseball officials ruled in 1887 that home plate would thereafter be made of rubber instead of the marble that previously had been used, and that the plate would be 12 inches square. In 1900 home plate was officially changed to its modern dimensions. Also MARBLE, PAN, PLATE, PLATTER, and SQUARE.

home plate umpire: See UMPIRE-IN-CHIEF.

homer: v. To hit a home run. Also DIAL 8, GO DEEP, GO DOWNTOWN, JACK ONE, PARK ONE, TAKE THE BALL DEEP, TAKE THE BALL DOWNTOWN, TAKE THE PITCHER DEEP, and TAKE THE PITCHER DOWNTOWN.
     n. A home run.

home run: n. A four-base hit, which scores the batter and any runners on base. Also CIRCUIT CLOUT, DINGER, DR. LONGBALL, DOWNTOWNER, FOUR BAGGER, FOUR-MASTER, FOUR-PLY POKE, HOMER, MOON SHOT, POKE, RAINBOW, ROUND-TRIPPER, SWAT, TAPE-MEASURE HOME RUN, and TATER.

home run in an elevator shaft: n. A high pop fly that goes straight up from home plate.

hook: n. 1. A curve ball. 2. The removal of a pitcher from a game. The word was borrowed from vaudeville Amateur Nights. When the theater manager decided an act was so bad that it had to be taken off the stage, he would extend a long hook from the wings and literally drag the performer off. See QUICK HOOK and PULL (2).

hook slide: See CHICAGO SLIDE.

Hoover: n. An infielder who "sweeps up" vitually every ball hit his way, much in the manner of a Hoover vacuum cleaner.

hop: n. 1. A bounce of a ground ball. 2. The sudden upward movement of a fastball as it approaches home plate. Also JUMP.

hopper: n. A ground ball that takes one or more high bounces.

horse-and-buggy league: n. A minor league. In general parlance, "horse and buggy" suggests something old and run-down, and thus of lesser quality. By the same token, a minor league is considered inferior to the majors.

horsehide: n. A baseball. Balls were wrapped in horsehide until cowhide become the covering of preference in 1974, and were sometimes referred to by their exterior surface, as in "Throw that old horsehide in here, boy!"

hose: n. A player's arm, especially the throwing arm.

hot corner: n. Third base, so named for the many hard-hit balls that come the third baseman's way. The phrase first appeared in print in 1889, when a Cincinnati writer noted that the Redlegs' third baseman had had a busy time "on the hot corner all afternoon and it's a miracle he wasn't murdered."

hot stove league: n. The winter months when major league baseball is not played, during which fans of the game proverbially sit around a hot stove and talk about seasons past and seasons to come.

House That Ruth Built, The: n. A nickname for Yankee Stadium in New York. When Babe Ruth joined the Yankees in 1920, the team played its home games in the Polo Grounds, traditionally the home park of the National League New York Giants. But because Ruth's tremendous batting exploits were drawing overflow crowds to the diminutive Polo Grounds, Yankee management decided to build a large stadium in the Bronx for the Yanks. It was officially opened in 1923, and unofficially dubbed "The House That Ruth Built," a play on the old rhyme "The House That Jack Built."

hummer: n. A fastball, a pitch thrown so hard that it seems to hum as it speeds toward home plate.

humpback liner: n. A line drive that quickly sails up and abruptly shoots down.

hung up: adj. phrase. Caught in a rundown, "hung up" between two fielders.

hurler: n. A pitcher.

ice cream cone: n. A catch made with the ball sticking out of the top of the glove so that it resembles a scoop of ice cream on a cone. Also SNOW CONE.

ice man: n. A reliever who comes into a game and "cools off" a hot-hitting batter or team. Also FIREMAN.

in-between hop: n. A hop, on a ground ball, that the defensive player fields immediately after the ball has bounced. Also SHORT HOP.

incurve: n. A curve ball that breaks toward the batter. Also INSHOOT.

indicator: n. A hand-held device used by the home plate umpire to monitor the number of balls, strikes, outs, and runs during a game. The indicator was first marketed by the A.G. Spalding Company in the 1880s, and in its earliest form recorded only balls and strikes.

infield: n. 1. The part of the playing field contained within the two foul lines and extending from home plate to the front edge of the outfield. In other words, this is the area of the field known as the diamond. 2. The defensive players who are positioned in the infield.

infielder: n. One of the four defensive players stationed near first, second, and third bases—the first, second, and third basemen, and the shortstop. See SACKER.

infield fly rule: n. A rule that declares the batter out when he hits a catchable fly ball into fair territory of the infield and there are less than two outs and first, first and second bases, or first, second and third bases are occupied by runners. In such a situation, an umpire immediately calls the ball an infield fly, thus declaring the batter out and warning the runners that they may advance at their own risk. The rule prevents infielders from purposely dropping a fly ball and then easily forcing the baserunners, who would ordinarily stay at their bases on an infield fly.

infield hit: n. A base hit on a batted ball that stays within the infield. A bunt hit and a swinging bunt hit are examples. Also SCRATCH HIT.

inning: n. A portion of the game when the two teams take their turns at bat. After the first team to bat has made three outs, then a half-inning is over, and the other team gets to bat. When each side has batted and made three outs, then an inning is completed. A game usually lasts until the losing team has been to bat in nine innings. In the first days of organized baseball, "inning" was borrowed from cricket, in which the word means a turn at bat for an individual batsman or an entire team. Also CANTO, FRAME, ROUND, and STANZA.

in play: prep. phrase. Refers to a thrown or batted ball that is in fair territory and playable. The expression was borrowed from the English sport of cricket during the mid-nineteenth century.

inshoot: See INCURVE.

inside baseball: n. The style of play in which the offensive team tries to score one run at a time through such tactics as the bunt, the steal, the hit-and-run, the well-placed hit, and the squeeze. So named because its action is confined to a limited portion of the playing field, inside baseball is said to have been perfected by the National League Baltimore Orioles of the 1890s. It was the dominant style of play until the 1920s, primarily because the "dead" ball then in use traveled only short distances when struck. After the introduction of the livelier "rabbit" ball around 1920, the home run became the prevalent method for scoring. Also SCIENTIFIC BASE-BALL.

inside-out swing: n. A swing that the batter makes with an open batting stance and his hands close to his body, usually resulting in a hit to the opposite field. Thus the batter is said to "inside-out the ball."

inside-the-park home run: n. A batted ball that stays within the boundaries of the playing field but allows the batter to circle the bases and make a home run. In baseball's early days, the outfield fences were so far back that a ball hit between two outfielders would roll a good distance and thus allow the batter to score. When outfield fences were brought closer to home plate, the frequency of inside-the-park homers decreased. During the early 1900s, some baseball writers referred to inside-the-park jobs as "bona fide" and "real" home runs, implying that they were harder to earn than balls lofted over the fence, and thus more qualified as home runs that had been rightfully earned.

insurance run: n. A run that adds to a team's lead in a game. A team usually tries for such a run when holding only a one- or two-run lead, but will settle for insurance tallies no matter what size the lead.

intentional base on balls, intentional walk: n. A base on balls that has been deliberately given to a batter as part of the defensive team's strategy. For instance, the defense may give an intentional base on balls to a powerful hitter so as to pitch against the weaker hitter who is next in the lineup. The intentional base on balls was not widely used in baseball strategy until the early 1900s.

interference: n. Obstruction by a player, an umpire, or a spectator with the action during a baseball game. "Offensive interference" is obstruction by a member of the offensive team with a defensive player's attempt to make a play. When the umpire has ruled the batter or runner out for interference, all other runners must return to the last base that was touched by the runners. "Defensive interference" is obstruction by a defensive player with a batter's attempt to hit a pitch. The most common offense in this category is catcher's interference, in which a catcher's glove touches a batter's bat during a swing. In that case, the batter is awarded first base by the home plate umpire. "Umpire interference" occurs when an ump hinders a catcher's attempt to throw out a baserunner who is trying to steal, or when a fair ball touches an umpire. "Spectator interference" happens when a fan reaches from his seat or goes on to the playing field and touches a ball that is in play. In all instances of interference, the ball is immediately ruled dead.

interleague play: n. A game, or games, between teams from the American and National Leagues. The only interleague play between the two leagues has taken place in pre-season and post-season contests, such as spring training exhibitions and the World Series. As far back as the early 1900s, some baseball writers and officials have suggested interleague games as part of the regular season schedule. But the game's powers-that-be have given the idea cursory consideration at best.

in the hole: See AT BAT.

IP: Abbreviation for "innings pitched."

iron hands: n. The hands of a fielder who frequently allows balls to bounce, or "clang," off his glove. Also HARD HANDS. See CLANG. Compare SOFT HANDS.

iron man: n. 1. A durable player, particularly one who appears in many consecutive games. Lou Gehrig is considered the all-time "iron man" for his record of 2,130 consecutive games played from 1925 to 1939. 2. A durable pitcher, particularly one who pitches many innings during a season and rarely misses a start. Joe McGinnity, a pitcher for the New York Giants at the turn of the century, was nicknamed "Iron Man" for pitching both games of a doubleheader five times. In August of 1903, he pitched and won both games of three doubleheaders. Also RUBBER ARM. 3. A ticket to a baseball game. In the game's early days, a ticket could be bought with a silver dollar, which was also known as an "iron man." 4. A baseball broadcaster, so called because announcers used microphones made of iron.

Iron Mike: n. A machine that throws pitches to hitters during batting practice. Primitive versions of the pitching machine were used in baseball as early as the 1890s, but Brooklyn Dodger President Branch Rickey popularized the Iron Mike after World War II. The machines are now able to throw almost any kind of pitch at varying speeds. Also PITCHING MACHINE.

ivory: n. A rookie, so called because a promising young player, like ivory, is a precious and actively sought commodity.

ivory hunter: n. A baseball scout. See IVORY.

jack one: v. To hit a home run, especially a prodigious homer.

jackrabbit ball: See RABBIT BALL.

jake, jaker: n. A player who often makes excuses to get out of playing, usually by claiming he has some sort of sickness or injury. The term is said to derive from a player with just such a reputation, Jake Stahl, an American Leaguer from 1903 to 1913. See ALBI IKE, CLUBHOUSE LAWYER, and PEBBLE PICKER.

Jawn Titus: n. A sensational fielding play, especially a catch of a fly ball. The term is a corruption of the name of John Titus, a talented outfielder for the Philadelphia Phillies at the turn of the century. Also CIRCUS CATCH.

jelly ball: n. A ball that a pitcher has illegally dabbed with grease or, a product preferred by more than a few modern hurlers, vaginal jelly.

John Anderson: n. An attempt to steal a base that is already occupied by another runner. For making such a gaffe while playing for the New York Highlanders (later the Yankees) in 1904, the name of John Anderson lives in baseball infamy.

John T. Brush Rules, The: See BRUSH RULES, THE.

journeyman: n. A veteran player who has been with several different teams during his career. Typical journeymen were "Suitcase Bob" Seeds, who played for six major league teams in nine seasons, and Harry "Suitcase" Simpson, who played for six teams in eight seasons. Kurt Bevacqua played for seven teams between 1971 and 1984 and accumulated only four seasons' worth of at bats.

Judy: See PUNCH-AND-JUDY HITTER.

jug, jug handle: n. A curve ball whose sharp break resembles both the outline and the handle of a jug.

juice: v. To hit a ball hard and far. Thus, a batter creates a lot of power or "juice."

jump: n. 1. A baserunner's first step in a stolen base attempt. 2. The movement on a good fastball, which seems to rise or "jump" as it crosses home plate. Also HOP.

junior circuit: n. A nickname for the American League. The name originated because the AL was founded 15 years after the other major league, the National League, which is also known as "the senior circuit." See AMERICAN LEAGUE.

junk: n. Many slow breaking pitches. The term is credited to baseball writer Ben Epstein of the *New York Daily Mirror,* who in 1948 first used "junk" to describe the type of pitches thrown by Eddie Lopat of the New York Yankees. Subsequently, Lopat and pitchers with a similar repertoire were called "junk men" or "junkballers." In 1983, after being collared by Baltimore Oriole junkballer Mike Boddicker, Rod Carew of the California Angels angrily remarked of Boddicker's pitches, "I take better stuff out to the garbage every night." Also PUFF BALL and SLOP.

K: n. 1. The shorthand symbol for a strikeout, used in box scores and in the scoring of games. The notation was introduced in 1868 by M.J. Kelly, a baseball writer for the *New York Herald*. Kelly avoided using "S," reasoning that people might think it stood for shortstop. He decided on "K" because it is the last letter in the word "struck." 2. A strike out.

kalsomine: n. A shutout, so called because calcimine—which some creative misspeller long ago turned into "kalsomine"—is a type of whitewash, and "whitewash" is a synonym for "shut out."

kangaroo ball: n. The lively baseball introduced to the game in 1920, which has been said to have as much jump and liveliness as a kangaroo. Also RABBIT BALL.

keystone: n. Second base, named because the foundation, or "keystone," of a good defensive team is having good fielders at second base and shortstop. See KEYSTONE COMBINATION.

keystone combination: n. A team's second baseman and shortstop. See KEYSTONE.

kick: n. The segment of a pitcher's throwing motion in which he raises, or "kicks," his leg.

v. 1. While pitching, to raise one's leg. 2. To make an error, in particular by literally kicking the ball. Also BOOT.

kimono pitch: n. A gimmick pitch devised in 1955 by New York Yankee hurler Tommy Byrne during a Yankee postseason exhibition tour of Japan. The southpaw Byrne threw his kimono pitch by bringing his throwing arm forward in a regular delivery motion but continuing to wheel his arm for one more revolution and then sending the slow arcing ball toward the surprised batter. When Byrne tried the pitch in an exhibition game against the Brooklyn Dodgers the following spring, home plate umpire Larry Napp called the pitch a "discard" and ordered Byrne not to throw it again. Delivered only one time in the major leagues—and during a spring training game, at that—the kimono ball is the only pitch to have been pronounced illegal in this century because of the pitcher's motion.

kitchen: n. The external area of the batter's chest. When a pitcher throws a high and tight fastball, he is said to be "coming into the batter's kitchen."

knock down: See BRUSH BACK.

knockdown pitch: See BRUSHBACK PITCH.

knock the pitcher out of the box: v. To get many hits and runs off a pitcher, causing him to leave the game and be relieved. The term dates from the late nineteenth century, when pitchers threw from a flat rectangular surface known as the "pitcher's box."

knothole gang: n. A program in which underprivileged youths are given free or discounted tickets to major league ball games. Baseball executive Branch Rickey is credited with introducing the "knothole gang" idea to the majors in the 1930s when he was general manager of the St. Louis Cardinals. However, Abner Powell, a minor league player–man-

KNOTHOLE GANG

ager of the late 1800s, reportedly invented the concept. Powell convinced his team's owner to give free seats to a group of kids who regularly watched games at New Orlean's Sportsman's Park through a hole in the wooden fence surrounding the ball yard. After Powell agreed to take responsibility for the children's behavior, the owner consented to admit them free to two games a week.

knuckle ball, knuckler: n. A pitch that is thrown by gripping the ball with the fingertips or fingernails and pushed toward home plate, and that is virtually spinless, its flight dictated mainly by the effect of air currents on the ball. Because no one throws a knuckle ball with his knuckles, the pitch is misnamed. Its origin is not clear, although some historians claim it was thrown as early as the 1880s. Also BUTTERFLY, FLOATER, and FLUTTERBALL.

knuckle curve: n. A curve ball thrown with the grip used for a knuckle ball.

krank: See FAN.

Ladies Day: n. A promotion in which women are admitted free to a baseball game if accompanied by a paying male customer. Considered the oldest baseball promotion, the Ladies Day concept was born on June 16, 1883, when all female customers received free admission to a game in New York between the homestanding Gothams and the Cleveland Spiders. (New York won, 5–2.) In 1889, Cincinnati became the first team to hold Ladies Days regularly when its officials noticed that considerably more women attended games when handsome Tony "The Count" Mullane pitched. National League officials abolished Ladies Day in 1909, fearing that the growing number of nonpaying female customers was not exactly helping business. Some American League clubs also did away with the promotion, though it made a comeback of sorts about 1920. In recent years, as women have become more avid spectators of sports in general, the promotion has become unnecessary and has virtually disappeared.

LaLob: n. The high, slow-arcing blooper pitch as named by its most recent practitioner, Dave LaRoche, who threw his LaLob in the early 1980s while working as a relief pitcher with the New York Yankees. Also BALLOON PITCH, BLOOPER PITCH, BUTTERFLY, and EPHUS.

Landis Line: n. The geographic line in the eastern United States, west or south of which no major league baseball teams could hold spring training from 1943 to 1945 because of war-time travel restrictions. Drawn by baseball commissioner Kenesaw Mountain Landis, the line was formed by the Potomac River to the south and the Mississippi River to the west. Instead of heading to their traditional training sites in the southern and western U.S., the 16 teams worked out during those three years in Illinois, Indiana, Missouri, New York, New Jersey, Maryland, Delaware, and Washington, D.C.

laugher: n. A game in which one team outscores the other by a laughably wide margin.

lawn mower: n. A sharply hit ground ball, a "grass cutter."

lay one down: v. To bunt. The term suggests the way a bunting batter is supposed to deaden the ball and gently send it rolling on the infield grass.

lead: n. A distance taken by a runner away from his current base, in preparation of either stealing the next base or having a running head start if the batter should hit the ball. See WALKING LEAD.
    v. To take a lead.

League Championship Series: n. The series between the Eastern and Western Division champions of each major league. Held immediately after the end of the regular season, the two series determine which teams will represent the American and National Leagues in the World Series. It is abbreviated as LCS and better known as the "playoffs." These series began in 1969, the first season in which the two leagues played in the divisional format. Through the 1984 season, the playoffs consisted of best-of-five series, but after the 1985 season, a best-of-seven format was adopted.

leather: 1. A baseball. The nickname dates from the game's early days when baseball coverings were make of leather. 2. Excellent defense, a reference to the players' leather gloves.

leatherman: n. An excellent fielder. Also GLOVE MAN.

left, left field: n. 1. The left portion of the outfield between center field and the left foul line. 2. A nickname for the left fielder.

left fielder: n. The defensive player positioned in left field. Also LEFT and LEFT FIELD.

left on base: adj. phrase. Refers to the number of runners that the offensive team leaves on base at the end of an inning. Abbreviated LOB. See STRAND.

lefty: n. A player who bats and/or throws left-handed. In addition, "Lefty" is probably the most common nickname in baseball history. Also PORTSIDER and SOUTHPAW.

leg hit: n. A hit that the batter makes by hitting a slow ground ball to the infield and beating the throw to first base. The batter can be said to have "legged out" the hit.

let-up pitch: n. A change-up, in which the pitcher slows down, or "lets up" on, the speed of a particular pitch. See CHANGE, CHANGE OF PACE, and CHANGE-UP.

lidlifter: n. The opening game of a doubleheader, a series, or a season. Also CURTAIN-RAISER.

life: n. A chance for a hitter to continue an at bat, especially after a fielder has dropped a foul ball or the catcher has failed to hold a foul tip that would have been the third strike. In this situation, the batter "has a life" or is "still alive."

light ball: n. A pitched or batted ball that has little spin and thus feels light to the player who catches it. Compare HEAVY BALL.

line drive, liner: n. A sharply hit ball with little arc. Also BLUE DARTER, CLOTHESLINE, CLOTHESLINER, DARTER, FROZEN ROPE, and ROPE.

lineup: See BATTING ORDER.

lineup card: n. A team's batting order for a particular game as written down on a card and presented to the home plate umpire before the game. Usually the managers of both teams will meet with all four umpires at home plate just before the start of the game to hand in lineup cards and discuss the ballpark's ground rules.

live arm: n. The arm of a player, particularly a pitcher, who throws with exceptional velocity.

live bat: n. 1. An excellent batter. 2. The bat of such a hitter.

live fastball: n. A fastball that jumps slightly as it crosses home plate and eludes the batter's swing.

load, load up: v. To put a substance illegally on the ball, which will give it a sharp break when pitched. Pitchers over the years have loaded balls up with spit, grease, mud, hair cream, sweat, and vaginal cream. See DOCTORED BALL.

location: n. A pitcher's ability to throw at exact spots around home plate.

lollipop: n. A pitch that's easy to hit. Also FAT PITCH and COOKIE. Compare CRIPPLE.

long man, long reliever: n. A relief pitcher who is called on to work several innings of a game, usually the middle innings between the early exit of the starting pitcher and the arrival late in the game of the short reliever. The longest relief job by a major league pitcher was 18⅓ innings by the Chicago Cubs' Zip Zabel in a 19-inning, 4–3 win over the Brooklyn Dodgers on June 17, 1915. Also MIDDLE MAN, MIDDLE RELIEVER, SETUP MAN, and SWING MAN.

long tater: See TATER.

looper: See TEXAS LEAGUER.

losing pitcher: See LOSS.

loss: n. The responsibility, noted officially in a pitcher's won–loss record, for allowing the runs that led to his team's losing a game. A starting pitcher is saddled with a loss when he leaves a game in which his team is trailing and never regains the lead. A relief pitcher gets a loss when he enters a game in which his team is tied or winning and he allows the run, or runs, that put the other team ahead for good. Compare WIN.

Louisville Slugger: n. The famous bat made by the Hillerich and Bradsby company, which had been based in Louisville, Kentucky, until moving in the early 1980s to the new Slugger Park complex in Jeffersonville, Indiana, eight miles from Louisville. The first Louisville Slugger was made by 18-year-old Bud Hillerich in the late 1800s for Pete "The Gladiator" Browning, a star hitter for the Louisville club of the American Association. Hillerich's new bat replaced the flat paddle-shaped model that Browning had been using before breaking it.

Lowdermilk: n. A pitcher who has poor control of his deliveries. The name comes from Grover Cleveland "Slim" Lowdermilk, a wild hurler who pitched for six teams in nine seasons during the early 1900s.

lumber: n. 1. A bat, the name deriving from the material used to make a bat. 2. A collective name for a team's lineup, particularly the lineup of a powerful team.

mace: n. A bat. In conventional English, a mace is a staff or a clublike weapon.

mackerel: n. A curve ball. The term originated when players observed long ago that a slow curve resembles a dead fish or, specifically, a dead mackerel.

major league: See BIG LEAGUE.

make the pivot: See TURN THE PIVOT.

man: See BASERUNNER.

manager: n. The nonplaying, uniformed coach who is responsible for running a team on the field. Usually stationed in the dugout, the manager makes out the starting lineup for each game, decides on changes during a game and flashes pitching and hitting signals. Also FIELD GENERAL, PILOT, SKIP, and SKIPPER.

marble: n. Home plate, so called because the plate was made of marble until baseball officials decreed in 1887 that home plate would thereafter be made of rubber. See HOME PLATE.

marked ball: n. A ball that a pitcher has illegally scuffed or scratched in order to make it break sharply when thrown. See DOCTORED BALL.

marker: n. A run, a word from the early years of the game.

matador: n. A player who tries to field a ball in the manner of a matador confronting a bull—that is, he jumps out of its path and waves at it.

meal ticket: n. The one player, especially a pitcher, who consistently performs well for his team. Such a player was pitcher Carl Hubbell, who earned the nicknames "King Carl" and "The Meal Ticket" while pitching for the New York Giants from 1928 to 1943.

meat hand: n. A fielder's bare hand, that is, the hand other than the one in his fielding glove.

meat of the bat: See FAT PART OF THE BAT.

meat of the batting order: n. The hitters in the three through five spots in the batting order, a team's most powerful batters. Presumably these hitters comprise the meat of the order because they offer the best "cuts."

Mendoza Line: n. A paltry batting average, usually one around .215, named in honor of Mario Mendoza, an infielder who played during the 1970s and early 1980s in the major leagues and annually posted anemic batting averages, such as .221, .180, .185, .198, and .218. A batter whose average dips to near .215, Mario's lifetime mark, is said to be "approaching the Mendoza Line." Kansas City Royal third baseman George Brett is credited with coining the phrase.

men in blue: n. Umpires, in general or a specific crew of umps, so called because their regulation outfit includes blue pants, a blue jacket, and a blue cap.

Merkle's Boner: n. Probably the most notorious blunder by a player in baseball history. Late in the 1908 season, the New York Giants and the Chicago Cubs were battling for the National League pennant. The two teams met in an important

September game, and going into the bottom of the ninth inning, the score was tied at 1–1. The homestanding Giants made two outs but got two men on base, Moose McCormick at third and rookie Fred Merkle at first. The next batter, Al Bridwell, lined the apparent game-winning hit into center field. As McCormick crossed home plate, Merkle ran halfway to second base and then, deciding to avoid the mob of Giant fans who were already rushing the playing field, took an abrupt right turn toward the clubhouse entrance in center field. Amid all the chaos, the Cubs got hold of a ball (which many Giants claimed was not even the game ball) and stepped on second base. The umpires ruled that Merkle was thus forced at second base, which technically nullified McCormick's winning run. The game was ruled a tie and had to be replayed later in the season. The Cubs won the replayed game—and the pennant— by one game over the Giants, who might have been the league champions had it not been for Fred Merkle's famous boner. Unfortunately for Merkle, this gaffe overshadowed his otherwise respectable 16-year playing career, in which he batted .273.

middle gardener: n. The center fielder, so called because the outfield has also been known as the "garden" and the center fielder is the man in the middle.

middle man: n. 1. The infielder who takes a throw from another fielder to force the first out in a double play. For example, in a 6–4–3 double play (the number 6 designating the shortstop, 4 the second baseman, and 3 the first baseman), the second baseman is the "middle man." Also PIVOT MAN. 2. See LONG MAN, LONG RELIEVER.

middle reliever: See LONG MAN, LONG RELIEVER.

Midsummer Classic: See ALL-STAR GAME.

minor league: n. A professional baseball league lower in rank than the two major leagues. Every major league club operates at least three minor league teams, which form that club's "farm system" or "minor league chain." The International Association, founded in Pittsburgh in 1877, was the first minor league. Before major league teams started operating minor league clubs, independent minor teams made money by selling players to interested big league squads. The initial affiliation between the major and minor leagues occurred in 1926, when St. Louis Cardinal general manager Branch Rickey organized a farm system for his club. Also BUSH LEAGUE, FARM, HAMBURGER LEAGUE, and HORSE-AND-BUGGY LEAGUE.

adj. Of or relating to the minor leagues.

Miracle of Coogan's Bluff: n. The pennant drive by the National League Champion New York Giants in 1951, a team that had been 13½ games behind the first-place Brooklyn Dodgers on August 11 and finished the season in a tie for first with Brooklyn. It is sometimes called "The Little Miracle of Coogan's Bluff" and "The Miracle at Coogan's Bluff." In the pennant-deciding best-of-three series that followed, the teams split the first two games. The Dodgers led the third game 4–1 in the bottom of the ninth inning when the home team Giants started to rally. They scored one run to make it 4–2. Then, with one out and two men on, Giant third baseman–outfielder Bobby Thomson hit reliever Ralph Branca's second pitch into the left field stands for the homer that won the game and the flag for New York. Thomson's home run, hit at 3:58 P.M. on October 3, 1951, was dubbed "The Shot Heard 'Round the World." Coogan's Bluff is the name of a cliff that stood behind the Giants' ballpark, the Polo Grounds.

mix up the pitches: v. To throw various pitches at various speeds to disrupt the batter's rhythm.

money player: n. A player who excels in clutch situations, one who earns his salary.

moon shot: n. A prodigious home run. The phrase came into popular use after the American moon excursions of the early 1970s.

mop-up man, mop-up reliever: n. A relief pitcher who is asked to enter the game after his team's starting pitcher has allowed a nearly insurmountable lead. Such a reliever must come in and "mop up" the mess left by the starter. A mop-up man is generally a second-line member of the bullpen staff. Also HAM-AND-EGG RELIEVER.

morning glory: n. A player, particularly a young one, who plays impressively early in the season but then fades as the year progresses. Also EARLY BLOOMER. Compare PHENOM.

morning journal: n. A bat made of bad wood, said to be as useless as a rolled newspaper. Also BANANA STICK. Compare PIECE OF IRON.

Most Valuable Player Award: n. An annual award given to the two most outstanding players in the American and National Leagues. Abbreviated MVP. Baseball first recognized its top players in 1911 when a Chalmers automobile was given to the best player in each league, Chicago's Frank Schulte in the National League and Detroit's Ty Cobb in the American. The Chalmers Award ended after 1914, and not until 1922 did a committee of American League officials give the first Most Valuable Player Award to George Sisler of the St. Louis Browns. A similar National League committee was formed in 1924. The AL committee failed to make a selection in 1929, and in 1930 neither league made a pick. The following year, 1931, the job of voting for the MVPs was handed over to the Baseball Writers Association of America, which has since voted every year for each circuit's best player.

mound: See PITCHER'S MOUND.

mow down: v. To retire the batting team easily, usually in three up, three down fashion. Also SET DOWN, and SKUNK. See ONE-TWO-THREE and THREE UP, THREE DOWN.

moxie: n. Tenacity, courage. Baseball is largely responsible for the introduction of this word to common parlance. Moxie was the name of a soft drink that became popular in New England during the early 1880s, primarily because it was sold at baseball games. The brand name was associated with courage because, the story goes, a good deal of it was required for swallowing the bitter-tasting liquid. Before long, "moxie" was applied to courageous ballplayers as well.

mud: n. A special concoction made from Delaware River mud and other secret ingredients, which umpires rub on a new baseball to remove slickness from the ball's surface. Russell "Lena" Blackburne, a major league player, coach, and manager in the early 1900s, was coaching third base for the Philadelphia Athletics one day when he overheard umpire Harry Geisel complain about the slick covering of a new ball. Blackburne remembered long ago using mud from a Delaware River tributary near his boyhood home to give a better grip to baseballs. During the ensuing winter, he dug up some mud from the Delaware and added a few other ingredients to smooth the mix. The next season he presented the finished product to Geisel, who was greatly pleased with its effectiveness and soon convinced umpires around the majors to use Blackburne's mud. Upon Lena Blackburne's death in 1968, the secret recipe was passed along to a friend, who later handed it down to his son-in-law. Before every major league game, umpires rub the mud on approximately 60 balls, 108 before a doubleheader.

mud ball: n. A pitched ball that has been illegally rubbed with mud in order to give the ball a more severe break as it approaches home plate. See DOCTORED BALL.

muff: v. To misplay a ball. Used as early as the 1860s, the word derives from "muffin," an earlier baseball term for a careless or an incompetent player.

Murderers' Row: n. A lineup consisting of many powerful hitters. Taken from the name of a section at The Tombs prison in New York, the term was first used by a baseball writer in

1858. "Murderers' Row" may be, and virtually has been, applied to any strong batting lineup, though the team most closely associated with the name is the 1927 New York Yankees. Widely regarded as one of the best all-around teams in baseball history, the 1927 Yankees included such hitters as Babe Ruth (.356 average, 60 home runs, 164 runs batted in), Lou Gehrig (.373, 47, 175), Bob Meusel (.337, 8, 103), Earle Combs (.356, 6, 64), Tony Lazzeri (.309, 18, 102), and Mark Koenig (.285, 3, 62).

mustard: n. A fastball, from the conventional slang term suggesting "zest." Often a pitcher will throw a fastball as a follow-up to a curve ball, which, of course, is putting mustard on a pretzel.

nail: v. 1. To put out a baserunner, especially on a tag play. 2. To hit a ball hard.

national anthem at baseball games: n. The custom of playing "The Star-Spangled Banner" before baseball games and other sporting events is said to have started at Wrigley Field in Chicago during the first game of the 1918 World Series between the Boston Red Sox and the Chicago Cubs. When the fans took their usual seventh-inning stretch, a band began playing "The Star-Spangled Banner," which was well-known at the time but not yet the national anthem. The Chicago fans spontaneously sang along and cheered loudly when the song was finished. It was played again at the next two Series games in Chicago and before the first game in Boston. Thereafter it was played before opening day and World Series games. The playing and singing of the anthem became standard practice during the 1940s, thanks to the patriotic fervor that came with World War II and the introduction of electronic public address systems to major league ballparks.

National Association: n. The first professional baseball league, formed in New York City on March 17, 1871. The charter teams were the Boston Red Stockings, the Chicago White Stockings, the Cleveland Forest Citys, the Fort Wayne Kekiongas, the New York Mutuals, the Philadelphia Athletics, the Rockford Forest Citys, the Washington Nationals and the Washington Olympics. A tenth charter club, the Brooklyn Eckfords, did not start that first season but joined in August 1871 to replace the folded Fort Wayne franchise. Originally a collection of amateur teams, the National Association lasted through the 1875 season. By then its image was tarnished by reports of gambling and bribery and the domination of the league by one team, the Red Stockings. In 1876 the best National Association players found work in a newly formed pro circuit called the National League. See NATIONAL LEAGUE.

National Baseball Hall of Fame and Museum: n. The shrine to baseball's finest players, managers, umpires, and executives, located in Cooperstown, New York. Founded in 1936 with the elections of Babe Ruth, Ty Cobb, Honus Wagner, Christy Mathewson, and Walter Johnson, the actual "hall" itself wasn't officially opened until 1939. Players and baseball writers initially voted on Hall of Fame candidates, but in the 1940s the balloting was turned over to the Baseball Writers Association of America. To be selected, a candidate must have ten years of major league experience and be listed on 75 percent of the ballots cast. No player is eligible until he has been retired for at least five years, although an exception was made in 1973 for Pittsburgh Pirate star Roberto Clemente, who died in a plane crash on December 31, 1972, while trying to help Nicaraguan earthquake victims. The Hall of Fame includes exhibits and a research library, and during the midsummer weekend when the latest inductees are enshrined, two major league teams play the Hall of Fame exhibition game in Cooperstown.

National Commission: n. The three-man group that ran baseball from 1903 until 1921, when Judge Kenesaw Mountain Landis was hired by the owners as the game's first single commissioner. The National Commission consisted of American League president Byron Bancroft "Ban" Johnson, National League president John K. Tener, and Cincinnati Reds owner August "Garry" Hermann. See COMMISSIONER OF BASEBALL.

National League: n. One of the two major leagues, the other being the American League. After corruption and the dominance of one team destroyed the first professional baseball league (see NATIONAL ASSOCIATION), would-be ballclub owners sought to create a circuit that would be more tightly run and feature a higher caliber of player. Led by Chicago businessman William A. Hulbert, they met at New York's Grand Central Hotel on February 2, 1876, and formed the National League. The charter teams were in Chicago, St. Louis, Hartford, Boston, Louisville, New York, Philadelphia, and Cincinnati. After the American League was founded in 1901 and had become an established major league, it was known as the "junior circuit" to the older National League, the "senior circuit." In 1969 each major league split into Eastern and Western Divisions, with the league champion determined by a best-of-five games series between the Eastern and Western Division winners. In 1985 those became a best-of-seven series.

national pastime: n. Baseball. While the game has been regarded as the American national pastime since the early 1900s, in recent decades Americans have shared their sporting passion with numerous other games, such as football, basketball, and hockey. More people may go to the horse track, and football may get better television ratings, but because it was our first national sport and has such a uniquely deep and story-filled past, baseball is still widely considered to be America's national pastime.

near beer pitcher: n. A pitcher who often works his way into counts of three balls and two strikes. Coined by Aaron Robinson, a New York Yankee catcher during the 1940s, the term alludes to near beer, a weakened type of brew that contains only 3.2 percent alcohol and is sometimes also called "3.2 beer."

Negro Leagues: n. The two six-club circuits of black baseball teams, known as the Negro American League and the Negro National League. The Negro Leagues formed in the early 1900s and started declining after Jackie Robinson broke major league baseball's color line by joining the Brooklyn Dodgers in 1947. Major league baseball reflected American society all too clearly in its refusal to let blacks play alongside whites, and thus blacks were forced to organize on their own. They played against Negro League rivals and all other comers, from amateur to semiprofessional, to raise the money that would keep the Negro teams afloat (and also to make a living). Records from Negro League games are sketchy, but enough is known so that great black stars such as Satchel Paige, Josh Gibson, Cool Papa Bell, Oscar Charleston, Judy Johnson, Buck Leonard, Marty Dihigo, and Pop Lloyd have been enshrined in the Hall of Fame in Cooperstown.

neighborhood play: n. A play in which the middle man in a double play, usually the shortstop or second baseman, fails to step on second base so as to avoid the sliding baserunner but is close enough for the umpire to call the out. Umpires use their discretion on this play. They allow the middle man to be "in the neighborhood" of the base because of the custom of some baserunners to slide in with their spikes high. Occasionally, however, if the middle man too obviously fails to touch the base, the ump will not call the out. Also PHANTOM DOUBLE-PLAY.

"Nice guys finish last": One of baseball's most famous utterances, spoken by Leo Durocher when he was managing the Brooklyn Dodgers during the 1946 season. Talking to reporter Frank Graham, Durocher pointed across the field to New York Giant manager Mel Ott and several Giant players. "All nice guys," Durocher supposedly said, "and they'll finish eighth." The line was altered, as original quotes often are, eventually becoming "Nice guys finish last," and has even been included in *Bartlett's Familiar Quotations*. Ironically, when Ott left the Giants' managerial spot after 78 games in 1948, his replacement was Leo Durocher, who led the team to a nice fifth-place finish.

nickel curve: n. A slider, so dubbed because it is considered a lesser brand of curve ball. See SLIDER.

NEIGHBORHOOD PLAY

night baseball: Baseball under lights dates to September 2, 1880, when teams from two Boston department stores played to a 16–16, nine-inning tie at Nantasket Bay, Massachusetts, in the first lighted night game. The contest was staged to demonstrate a new outdoor lighting display by the Northern Electric Light Company of Boston. During the next 50 years, several night games were played, but mainly as demonstrations of lighting techniques and the possibilities of nocturnal baseball. By the early 1930s, many minor league parks were equipped with lights, and not coincidentally, attendance at bush league games greatly increased despite the Depression. The major league hierarchy, traditionally slow to innovate, was reluctant to experiment with night games, but the first night game in the major leagues was finally played at Cincinnati's Crosley Field on May 24, 1935, as the Reds beat the Philadelphia Phillies 2–1. The first American League park to install lights was Philadelphia's Shibe Park in 1939. A year later, only 6 of the 16 big league stadiums were not equipped with lights. By the end of the 1940s, every ballpark except Chicago's Wrigley Field had lights. At this writing, Wrigley remains unlighted, the sole park in the majors where only day games are played. The first All-Star Game played at night was on July 6, 1942, at New York's Polo Grounds, where the American League beat the National 3-1. The first season-opening game at night took place on April 18, 1950, at Sportsman's Park in St. Louis, as the Cardinals won 4–2 over the Pittsburgh Pirates. Three decades later, on October 13, 1971, the Pirates were involved in the first World Series night game, defeating the Baltimore Orioles 4–3 in game four of the series at Pittsburgh's Three Rivers Stadium.

nightcap: n. The second game of a doubleheader. The word comes from the custom of having one last drink, a "nightcap," before leaving a bar or going to bed. Also AFTERPIECE.

nine: n. A baseball team, specifically the nine players (ten with the designated hitter) in a starting lineup. Alexander Cartwright, the father of modern baseball, established that a side would consist of nine players. In the first game played under Cartwright's modern rules, on June 19, 1846, at Elysian Fields in Hoboken, New Jersey, Cartwright's Knickerbockers lost to a team called the New York Nine.

no-hit: v. To hold hitless, as in "The pitcher was determined to no-hit the other team."

no-hitter, no-no: n. A game in which a team's pitcher or pitchers allow no base hits by the other team. The first recorded no-hitter in professional baseball was pitched in National Association play on July 28, 1875. Joe Borden of Philadelphia twirled his masterpiece against Chicago, winning 4–0.

nubber: n. A weakly hit ball that usually stays in the infield. The word comes from "nub" or "nubbin," meaning something small and undeveloped.

number one: n. A fastball, for which a catcher signals by wagging one finger to the pitcher.

number two: n. A curve ball. When a catcher wags two fingers, he is signaling for the pitcher to throw a curve.

occupy the points: v. To form the battery, one point being the pitcher, the other being the catcher. The expression dates from the late 1800s. See BATTERY.

ofer: adj. Hitless, as in "0 for 5." When a batter has gone without a hit in a game or in a series of games, he is said to have gone "ofer." See COLLAR.

off field: n. The part of the field opposite from where the batter stands in the batter's box. Off field for a right-handed batter is right field, left field for a lefty batter. Also OPPOSITE FIELD and WRONG FIELD.

official scorer: n. A person, usually a baseball reporter, who sits in the press box and serves as scorekeeper, determining when to call a particular play an error, a base hit, a passed ball, a wild pitch, and so on.

off-speed pitch: See CHANGE, CHANGE OF PACE, and CHANGE-UP.

off the schneid: An expression of Yiddish origin referring to a player or a team that has finally scored after being shut out for a lengthy period. Baseball broadcasters and writers sometimes use the phrase to describe the first hit by a player, or the first run by a team, etc., in many attempts: "With that base hit, he's finally off the schneid." In the garment district of New York, a "schneider" was a boss's term of derision for a cloth-cutter. When the garment bosses got together to play gin rummy, they called a hapless player who scored no points a "schneider." Once the player scored, he was said to get "off the schneider" or "off the schneid."

Old Oriole: n. A feisty, hard-nosed player. The Baltimore Orioles who played in the National League during the 1890s, called the Old Orioles after Baltimore was later represented by teams known as the Orioles in the American and International Leagues, were tough players who used methods legal and sometimes less-than-legal to scratch out runs.

Old-Timers' Day: n. A promotion in which retired ballplayers take part in an introduction ceremony and a short game before a regular major league game. George Weiss established the first Old-Timers' Day during the early 1940s while serving as general manager of the New York Yankees. The idea evolved from the practice, which went as far back as the early 1900s, of asking a retired star to play all or part of an actual game as a promotional gimmick.

on-base average, on-base percentage: n. A statistic that reflects a player's ability to reach base. To figure a player's on-base percentage, divide the number of times he reaches base by the number of his plate appearances (which include at bats, bases on balls, times hit by the pitch, and times interfered with by the catcher). A familiar stat, though one not officially kept by the major leagues, on-base percentage first drew wide attention in the 1950s. Baseball writers and officials used a primitive form of on-base average, known as Reached First Base, in 1879, and then scrapped it.

on deck: adj. Waiting to bat next, from the nautical expression "on deck," or ready for duty. To help speed up games, a rule was passed in the early 1960s requiring the next hitter to be positioned on the field in the on-deck circle. See AT BAT and ON DECK CIRCLE.

on deck circle: n. A circular area near each team's dugout, in which the next hitter waits for his turn to bat. See ON DECK.

one-cushion shot: n. A ball that caroms once off the outfield wall. The term derives from billiards.

one o'clock hitter: n. A batter who hits well in pregame batting practice but poorly in the game itself. This term derives from the days when baseball games were started about 3 P.M. and batting practice was held about 1 P.M. Nowadays, with most games beginning in the evening, such a batter is labeled a "seven o'clock hitter."

one, two, three: A phrase used to describe an inning in which only three players batted and all made outs. Also THREE UP, THREE DOWN. See MOW DOWN, SET DOWN, and SKUNK.

on the fists: Refers to a pitch thrown near the batter's fists, the strategy being that he cannot extend his bat on such a pitch. If he does hit the ball, he usually will produce only a weak ground ball or a weak pop-up.

open stance: n. A batting stance in which the batter's front foot is closer than his back foot to the lengthwise side of the batter's box farther from home plate, thus leaving the front of his body "open" to the pitcher. Compare CLOSED STANCE and PARALLEL STANCE.

opposite field: See OFF FIELD.

orchard: n. 1. The outfield. Also GARDEN and PASTURE.

orchardman: n. An outfielder, so named because he plays in the outfield, also known as the "orchard."

outcurve: n. A curve ball that breaks away from the batter. Also OUTSHOOT.

outfield: n. The area of the playing field between the back edge of the infield and the rear wall of the ballpark. Also GARDEN, ORCHARD, and PASTURE.

outfielder: n. One of the three defensive players—the right fielder, the center fielder, and the left fielder—who patrol the outfield. Also GARDENER, ORCHARDMAN, and PASTURE WORKER.

out in front: adj. Swinging the bat well before the ball arrives at the plate.

out man: n. A batter who is easy to get out. Also EASY OUT. Compare TOUGH OUT.

out pitch: n. A pitcher's best pitch, the one he relies on most to get batters out. Also BREAD-AND-BUTTER PITCH.

outshoot: See OUTCURVE.

outside: adj. Outside of the strike zone, beyond the side of the plate opposite the batter. Also AWAY.

over the top: v. To throw or pitch by bringing the throwing arm over the head, in contrast to sidearm or underhand throwing. The overhand pitching motion was legalized in 1884.

overtime: n. Extra innings. Baseball broadcasters and writers sometimes use this expression, borrowing it from clocked sports such as football and basketball. However, it seems ill-suited to baseball, among whose charms is the absence of a clock. If baseball doesn't have time, how can it have overtime?

paint the black: v. To throw pitches consistently that pass over the black edges of home plate for strikes. Also SHAVE THE CORNERS.

palm ball: n. An off-speed pitch that has little spin and breaks sharply and unpredictably as it nears home plate, much like a knuckle ball. The ball is gripped between the thumb and the palm—thus its name.

pan: See HOME PLATE.

pancake: n. A flat glove, especially the old unpadded mitts that players wore until about the 1920s. See FIELDING GLOVE.

parachute: n. A high fly ball that falls between the infielders and the outfielders, similar to, but with a higher arc than, a BLOOP, BLOOPER, DYING QUAIL, FLARE, QUAIL, QUAIL SHOT, TEXAS LEAGUER, or WOUNDED DUCK.

park one: v. To hit a home run, to "park one (the ball) in the stands."

parallel stance: n. A batting stance in which the batter's feet form a line parallel to the side of home plate. Also SQUARE

STANCE and STRAIGHT STANCE. Compare CLOSED
STANCE and OPEN STANCE.

pass: n. 1. A base on balls, a "free ticket" to first base. See
BASE ON BALLS.
    v. to give a batter a base on balls.

passed ball: n. A pitched ball that eludes the catcher and
allows the baseunner or baserunners to advance. The official
scorer rules a passed ball when he deems that the catcher
should have caught the ball. Compare WILD PITCH.

pasture: n. The outfield. Also GARDEN and ORCHARD.

pasture worker: n. An outfielder, who works the outfield or
"pasture."

payoff pitch: n. A pitch with a count of three balls and two
strikes. Unless fouled off, this pitch must "pay off" in a base
on balls, a strike out, or a batted ball in play. Also THREE-
TWO PITCH.

pea: n. A baseball, especially a ball batted or thrown so hard
that it appears as small as a pea.

pebble picker: n. An infielder who often blames his errors
on pebbles in the infield dirt. See ALIBI IKE, CLUBHOUSE
LAWYER, JAKE, and JAKER.

peg: n. A throw, particularly a long throw in an attempt to
make a put-out.

Peggy Lee fastball: n. A derisive name for a weak fastball.
Coined by relief pitcher Tug McGraw during the mid-1970s,
the term came from a popular song, "Is That All There Is?,"
sung by Peggy Lee. Players have since adapted the expression to deride other pitches—a "Peggy Lee curve," a "Peggy
Lee slider," a Peggy Lee change-up," and so on.

pennant: n. A league championship. The championship of a league division is sometimes called a "half-pennant." Also FLAG and GONFALON.

pepper: n. 1. A batting and fielding excerise in which one or more fielders stand several feet away from a batter. One of the fielders tosses a ball to the batter, who hits it back with a short downward swing. Years ago fans often came early to ballparks to watch the more elaborate, almost acrobatic pepper games players put on, but in the 1950s pepper was banned from the parks because players sometimes damaged the field in their boisterousness, and also because it was feared that a stray ball might injure a spectator. 2. A fastball or many fastballs. 3. Enthusiasm, spirit.
    v. To hit a ball hard, particularly for a line drive.

percentage baseball: n. A style of baseball in which the manager makes the standard traditional moves, or plays by "The Book." For example, when the other team brings in a left-handed relief pitcher, a manager who plays "percentage baseball" will usually send up a right-handed pinch-hitter. Also BOOK, THE.

perfect game: n. A game in which one team's pitcher or pitchers do not allow any member of the opposition to reach first base in any way. The first perfect game in professional baseball was thrown by John Richmond of the National League Worcester club on June 12, 1880. He defeated Cleveland 1–0. Five days later, John M. Ward of Providence, also a National League team, hurled a 5–0 perfect game against Buffalo.

phantom double-play: See NEIGHBORHOOD PLAY.

phenom (also spelled "pheenom"; pronounced FEE-nom): n. A young player of "phenomenal" potential. Sometimes phenoms live up to their advance billing, but often they do not, perhaps crumbling under the pressure of the high expectations of others. The word was introduced in the late

1940s by sportswriter Garry Schumacher, who applied it to a New York Giant prospect named Clint Hartung. However, as a pitcher–outfielder, Hartung developed into a mediocre major leaguer at best, winning 29 games and losing 29, and hitting .238 over six seasons. Compare EARLY BLOOMER and MORNING GLORY.

pick it: v. To field deftly. A good fielder, it is said, "can really pick it."

pickle: n. A rundown, from the colloquial expression "in a pickle," meaning in a difficult situation.

pick-off move: n. The act of a pitcher's turning and throwing to a base, usually first base, in an attempt to put out a runner who is taking a lead.

pick up the runner: v. To drive in a baserunner.

piece of iron: n. An excellent bat, so named in baseball's early days when players often would drive nails and other bits of metal into their bats to make them more powerful. Compare BANANA STICK and MORNING JOURNAL.

pill: n. A baseball thrown or hit with such great velocity that it seems as small as a pill.

pilot: n. A field manager of a baseball team. See MANAGER.
    v. To manage.

pinch-hit: v. To bat during a game in the place of another batter. While the batter being replaced cannot return to the game, the pinch-hitter may stay, replacing either the batter for whom he hit or another player. Pinch-hitting did not become a regular part of baseball strategy until the early 1900s. In fact, in 1876 the National League had a rule against any substitutions before the fourth inning. John Doyle of the Cleveland Spiders became the first major leaguer to pinch bat, and got a hit in his lone attempt in 1892. That same year baseball writer Charlie Dryden invented the term "pinch hit," explaining that the batter came up in a "pinch," or a difficult situation. The first player to be used regularly as a pinch hitter was the St. Louis Browns' Dode Criss, who was 12 for 41 in pinch hit at bats in 1908. Pinch-hitting is a difficult art in that it involves coming off the bench into a tense game situation with virtually no warm-up. The all-time leader in pinch hits is Manny Mota, who played in the National League from 1962 to 1980 and made 150 hits in a pinch.

pinch hit: n. A hit made by a batter who is pinch-hitting.

pinch hitter: n. A batter who enters a game to bat for a teammate. Once replaced, a player is out of the game. See PINCH-HIT.

pinch-run: v. To run during a game in the place of another baserunner. The runner being replaced cannot return to the game.

pinch runner: n. A player who enters the game to run the bases for a teammate. Once replaced, a player is out of the game.

pine-tar ball: n. A ball that has been secretly and illegally rubbed with pine tar to make it break severely when thrown by a pitcher. See DOCTORED BALL.

pine-tar towel: n. A towel covered with pine tar that players rub on their bat handles to get a better grip. The towel is usually kept in the on-deck circle during a team's at bat.

pitch: v. To serve as the defensive player known as the pitcher, who stands on a mound 60 feet and six inches from home plate and delivers the ball to the batter.
    n. A delivery thrown by the pitcher.

pitch around the batter: v. To pitch carefully to an outstanding batter, giving him pitches that he would be unlikely to hit well. Pitching around a dangerous hitter often results in a base on balls, but most pitchers would rather walk a good hitter than let him hit a ball out of the park.

pitcher: n. 1. The defensive player who stands on the pitcher's mound 60 feet and six inches away from home plate and delivers the ball to the batter. Also BOXMAN, CHUCKER, FLIPPER, HEAVER, HURLER, SLAB ARTIST, SLABBER, SLABBIST, TOSSER, and TWIRLER. 2. The position played by the pitcher. 3. A pitcher who throws a variety of pitches at a variety of speeds, in contrast to a "thrower," who tries to overcome the batter with little else but fastballs. Also CONTROL PITCHER and FINESSE PITCHER. Compare POWER PITCHER.

pitcher of record: n. One of the two pitchers credited with a decision in a game, either the win or the loss.

pitcher's best friend: n. A double play, so named because it gets the pitcher out of many jams. Also TWIN KILLING.

pitcher's box: n. The flat, four-sided area from which the pitcher threw before the introduction of the pitcher's mound in 1903. The pitcher's box was based on the bowler's box in the English game of rounders. In 1863 the pitcher's box measured 12 feet by 4 feet, and the pitcher had to keep both feet on the ground while throwing. The box was made 12 feet square in 1867, and the pitcher was allowed to move at will in his delivery. In 1884, Providence pitcher Charles "Old Hoss" Radbourn used a running start like that of a cricket bowler and won 60 games. Four feet by five and one-half feet became the measurements of the box in 1887, and in 1893, the year the pitching distance was changed from 50 feet to 60 and one-half feet, the box was eliminated and replaced by a rubber slab, against which the pitcher had to keep his rear foot while throwing to the plate. The pitcher's box was marked off with an iron quoit at each corner. A ball hit past the pitcher was said to go "through the box," and when a pitcher gave up so many hits and runs that he had to leave the game, he was "knocked out of the box." Both expressions are still in use, even if the pitcher's box is not. See also PITCHER'S MOUND and PITCHER'S RUBBER.

pitchers' duel: n. A game in which both teams' pitchers hold the opposition to few hits and runs. Most baseball aficionados love a good pitchers' duel for its tension, sterling defense, and outstanding work by the hurlers. Baseball lore is filled with great pitchers' duels, but three are especially noteworthy. On May 2, 1917, at Chicago's Wrigley Field (not exactly a pitcher's haven), Jim Vaughn of the Chicago Cubs and Fred Toney of the Cincinnati Reds faced each other, and after nine innings, each man had a no-hitter. In the tenth inning, the Reds got a hit and a run off Vaughn, and Toney held on in the bottom of the frame to pick up a 1–0 no-hitter. Almost exactly three years later, on May 1, 1920, Joe Oeschger of the Boston Braves pitched against Leon Cadore of the Brooklyn Dodgers. Both men worked all 26 innings of a 1–1 tie. In that game, nearly the equivalent of three full contests, Oeschger gave up nine hits, four walks, and struck out seven, while Cadore allowed fifteen hits, five walks, and also fanned seven. On September 9, 1965, Bobby Hendley of the Chicago Cubs threw a one-hitter against the Los Angeles Dodgers but was beaten 1–0 by Sandy Koufax's perfect game.

pitcher's mound: n. The rounded dirt hill from which the pitcher makes his deliveries. He works with his rear foot on the pitcher's rubber, which sits at the center of the mound and is 60 and one-half feet from home plate. The mound was introduced to major league baseball in 1903, and was set at no more than 15 inches above the base lines and home plate. In 1969, after pitchers had thoroughly dominated hitters during the previous season, the peak of the mound was lowered to a height of 10 inches. Also HILL and MOUND. See PITCHER'S BOX and PITCHER'S RUBBER.

pitcher's rubber: n. The 24-inch-by-6-inch rubber slab placed atop the pitcher's mound and against which the pitcher must keep his rear foot while throwing to home plate. The front of the rubber is 60 feet and 6 inches from the back corner of home plate. The rubber was introduced in 1893 and was originally 12 inches by 6 inches. Two years later it was enlarged to its present size. Also RUBBER and SLAB. See PITCHER'S BOX and PITCHER'S MOUND.

pitching chart: n. A chart that makes note of each pitch thrown during a game—the type of pitch, its location, whether and where it was hit. The pitcher who is scheduled to start the next game usually keeps the pitching chart during a game. Brooklyn Dodger general manager Branch Rickey introduced the pitching chart in the late 1940s, hiring a statistician from the Montreal Canadians hockey team, Alan Roth (later a baseball statistician for American television), to sit behind home plate at Dodger games and "chart" each pitch. The practice did not become common in the majors until about 1960.

pitching machine: See IRON MIKE.

pitch-out: n. A fastball deliberately thrown extremely high to and away from the batter so that the catcher can grab the ball and make a throw in an attempt to put out a runner who is trying to steal a base. The catcher or a coach from the defensive team will signal for a pitch-out when he suspects that the baserunner will attempt to steal on the next pitch.
    v. To make a pitch out.

pivot man: See MIDDLE MAN.

plate: See HOME PLATE.

plate umpire: See UMPIRE-IN-CHIEF.

platoon: n. A reserve player, one who is usually not a starter.

v. To use players on a platoon basis.

adj. Of or relating to the platoon system of managing players.

platter: See HOME PLATE.

player endorsement: n. The appearance of a player's name or image in an advertisement for a commercial product. An easy way of making extra money, player endorsements began in the late 1800s when ballplayers appeared on cards (forerunners of the modern baseball card) that came in cigarette packs. Ty Cobb and Larry Lajoie endorsed Coca-Cola, while Dazzy Vance let his name be used in an ad for "Grandstand Green" paint and Smokey Joe Wood peddled shoes. Over the years ballplayers have worked as spokesmen for products ranging from chewing gum to automobiles. A superstar can make more money from endorsements than he can from his salary as a player.

player–manager: n. A player who also serves as his team's manager. Player–managers over the years have included John McGraw, Connie Mack, Miller Huggins, Bucky Harris, Tris Speaker, Ty Cobb, Rogers Hornsby, Bill Terry, Gabby Hartnett, Frankie Frisch, Joe Cronin, Mickey Cochrane, Lou Boudreau, Frank Robinson, Joe Torre, and Pete Rose. Because modern baseball has become so specialized and the problems of running a club more complex, owners prefer to hire men who will concentrate only on managing and not on their own hitting and fielding. Thus, the number of player–managers has dwindled dramatically over the years.

Players' League: n. A professional baseball league that was organized by former major leaguers and lasted for only the 1890 season. Five years after forming a union known as the Brotherhood of Professional Ball Players, members of teams from the National League and the American Association, then the two major leagues, decided they had had enough of what they considered injustices by the club owners—low salaries, gratuitous fines, the reserve clause—and formed their own league, aptly named the Players' League. They founded franchises in towns, or their environs, that already had clubs in the National League or American Association: Boston, Brooklyn, New York, Chicago, Philadelphia, Pittsburgh, Cleveland, and Buffalo. Wrecked by poor organization and high salaries, the Players' League folded after one season and its members were allowed to rejoin their old teams without penalty. The uprising did little to resolve any of the players' complaints, only exacerbating the sour relationship between the owners and their employees.

player to be named later: n. An undetermined player in a trade. For example, two trading clubs may make a deal in which one club agrees to send a player to the other club. They will eventually decide who that player will be, but when the deal is announced, the two clubs will say that it involves "a player to be named later."

playoff: n. A game or series of games to determine a league or divisional champion. Before both major leagues adopted the divisional format in 1969, the National League broke a regular season-ending deadlock for first place by holding a best-of-five playoff, while the American League would stage a one-game winner-take-all contest. In case of a tie for first in a division, the teams meet in a one-game playoff.

playoffs: See LEAGUE CHAMPIONSHIP SERIES.

plugged bat: n. An illegally doctored bat that has been hollowed near the head and filled with a light material such as cork. This makes the bat lighter while the mass of the bat—the hitting part—is unaffected. Also CORKED BAT. See DOCTORED BAT.

pneumonia ball: n. The name that players gave to the fastball thrown by Walter Johnson, the great Washington Senator pitcher of the early 1900s. Batters called it a "pneumonia ball" because they said they felt a blast of cold air after the ball rushed by them. This term contrasts with the many expressions that suggest the heat generated by a good fastball—for example, "steam," "blazer," "smoke," "mustard," and "pepper."

poke: n. A batted ball that travels a great distance, usually for a home run.

pole: n. 1. A bat. 2. See FOUL POLE.
    v. to hit a ball hard.

pop: n. A fly ball that generally stays within the infield. Also POP FLY, POPPER and POP UP.
    v. To hit a pop. Also POP UP.

pop fly: See POP (n.).

pop-out: n. A pop that is caught by a fielder for an out.
    v. To hit a pop-out.

popper: See POP (n.).

pop up: See POP (n. and v.).

pop-up slide: n. A slide in which the runner immediately stands or "pops" up after reaching a base. Also STAND-UP SLIDE.

portsider: n. A left-handed player, from the nautical term for the left side of a boat. Also LEFTY and SOUTHPAW.

position: n. 1. The particular area in which a fielder stations himself. 2. A batter's spot in the batting order.

PNEUMONIA BALL

v. To adjust to a certain area of the field. For instance, when a left-handed pull hitter comes to bat, the defensive players on the right side of the field will usually "position" themselves closer to the right field foul line.

postseason: n. The period following the regular season, during which play-off, league championship, and World Series games are played.

potato: n. A baseball.

powder: v. To hit a ball hard—figuratively speaking, to turn it into powder.

powder-puff ball: n. An illegal pitch, in which the ball has been surreptitiously coated with resin powder or flour and creates a distracting white cloud as it nears home plate. Gaylord Perry, the wily wizard of the doctored pitch, is credited with devising the powder-puff ball. Also PUFF BALL.

power alley: n. See ALLEY.

power hitter: n. A hitter who regularly makes extra-base hits, particularly home runs.

power pitcher: n. A pitcher who relies primarily on fastballs to get batters out, mainly by striking them out. Power pitchers over the years have included Walter Johnson, Bob Feller, and Nolan Ryan. Also THROWER. Compare CONTROL PITCHER, FINESSE PITCHER, and PITCHER (3).

pretzel: n. A curve ball that twists and turns much like a pretzel. Then again, many batters have twisted themselves into pretzel-like shapes while trying to hit curve balls.

program: See SCORECARD.

protect the line: See GUARD THE LINE.

PRETZEL

protect the plate: See GUARD THE PLATE.

protect the runner: v. To swing at a pitch on which a runner attempts to steal a base. The batter's swing blocks the catcher's vision and delays his attempt to throw out the runner.

protest: n. Notification of the umpire by a manager that, because of a disagreement over a call, he is playing the game "under protest." According to procedure, the protest is then reviewed by the president of the league, who then decides whether he allows or overrules the protest. If he allows the protest, then the president must determine how the ruling would affect the game in question. If the protest is overruled, then the game goes into the record books. More often than not, protests are overruled. In fact, they are allowed almost as infrequently as games get snowed out in the Houston Astrodome.

puff ball: n. 1. A derisive term for a slow breaking pitch. Batters label such a pitch a "puff ball" because, in their opinion, it does not challenge them the way a fastball does. 2. See POWDER-PUFF BALL.

pull: v. 1. To hit a ball toward the side of the field on which the batter is hitting. See PULL HITTER. 2. To remove a player, especially a pitcher, from a game. See HOOK and QUICK HOOK.

pull a Brenagan: v. To be struck on the hands by a ball. Sam Brenagan's big league career consisted of catching one game with Pittsburgh in 1914. With a man on third in that game, Brenagan was struck on the thumb by a pitch. The ball rolled away, and instead of chasing it, Sam shook his hand in pain as the man from third scored. The former minor leaguer was soon back in the minors to stay, but for years afterward, whenever a player was hit on the hand, he was said to be "pulling a Brenagan."

pull a Casey: See "CASEY AT THE BAT" and DO A CASEY.

pull an Exorcist: v. To look over your shoulder at the play behind you while running the bases. The phrase derives from the film *The Exorcist* in which a young girl possessed by the devil is able to turn her head completely around. Kurt Bevacqua of the San Diego Padres used this expression during the 1984 World Series between the Padres and the Detroit Tigers. "I wasn't pulling an Exorcist and checking the relay," Bevacqua told reporters, meaning that he was not looking over his shoulder at the relay from right field while he was rounding second base on a hit that he tried unsuccessfully to turn into a triple in game one of the Series. "Pull an Exorcist" is not yet a standard baseball expression, but maybe it should be.

pull-down sunglasses: n. Sunglasses that fit beneath the bill of a player's cap and can be pulled down, or pushed up, as needed. Fred Clarke, a National League outfielder from 1894 to 1915, is credited with this invention. Also FLIP GLASSES.

pull hitter: n. A batter who tends to hit, or "pull," the ball toward the side of the field on which he bats. A right-handed batter would "pull" toward left field, a left-handed batter toward right field.

pull the string: v. To throw a change-up. To the batter who swings too early at an off-speed pitch, the pitcher seems to have "pulled a string" and yanked the ball away.

pull the trigger: v. To swing tentatively at a pitch but far enough around for the home plate umpire to rule it a swing, and thus charge the batter with a strike. Also BREAK THE WRISTS, COMMIT ONESELF, and GO AROUND.

pump: n. The part of a full wind-up by a pitcher during which he raises his arms backward and then forward over his head.

punch: n. Hitting ability. A good-hitting player or team has "a lot of punch."

Punch-and-Judy hitter, punch hitter: n. A hitter who takes short compact swings, or "punches," at the ball, in contrast to a slugging-type hitter who takes wide and powerful cuts. Also JUDY.

punch out: v. 1. To strike out a batter. The term derives from boxing, in which one fighter "punches out" the other.

purpose pitch: n. A pitch that is meant to back the batter away from the plate. "That was a purpose pitch," baseball executive Branch Rickey once said, "the purpose being to separate the batter's head from his shoulders." See BRUSH-BACK PITCH.

push-button manager: n. The manager of a talented team. All he's expected to do is sit back, "push the buttons," and watch his club win. The term is sometimes a put-down, implying that anyone could manage such a team.

putout: n. The act of retiring an offensive player, such as by striking out a batter, causing a batter to fly out, forcing a runner at a base, tagging out a runner who is attempting to steal, and so on. A putout is credited to the defensive player who tagged a runner, touched a base to force a runner, or caught a fly ball. The catcher is credited with a putout when he tags a runner out at home plate or catches a third strike or when the batter obstructs the catcher and is therefore called out, stands out of the batter's box while hitting, bats in the wrong order, or bunts foul with two strikes. When the runner is put out because he was hit by a batted ball or interfered with a fielder, then the defensive player closest to the play or the player who would have made the play if unobstructed is credited with the putout.

put out: v. To cause a player on the other team to make an out. "Put out" is derived from the English games of cricket and rounders. Also RETIRE.

put the ball in play: v. To hit a ball into fair territory so that a play must be made by the defensive team.

quail, quail shot: See DYING QUAIL.

quick hook: n. A manager's tendency to take a pitcher out of a game at the slightest sign of a prolonged threat by the offensive team. When Sparky Anderson was managing the Cincinnati Reds in the 1970s, he removed his pitchers so quickly that he earned the nickname "Captain Hook." See HOOK and PULL.

quick pitch: n. 1. An illegal pitch thrown before the batter is completely set and comfortable in the batter's box. If thrown with no runners on base, the pitch is ruled a ball. If a quick pitch is made with one or more runners on base, a balk is called. 2. A legal pitch made with no wind-up. (This is a legal pitch, in contrast to the one defined above, because the pitcher waits until the batter is set before delivering the ball.) In recent years, journeyman pitcher Jim Kaat often used the legal quick pitch. Also QUICK-RETURN PITCH.
    v. To throw a quick pitch.

quick-return pitch: See QUICK PITCH.

rabbit: n. 1. A player who runs fast. Also SPEED MER-
CHANT. 2. The liveliness of the baseball introduced to the
game in the early 1920s, as in "The ball has a lot of rabbit in
it." See RABBIT BALL.

rabbit ball: n. The lively ball that the American League
began using in 1920, the National League in 1921. Baseball
team owners decided to use the ball, which traveled faster
and farther when hit than did the old ball, to generate more
offense and, so they reasoned, more fan interest in the game.
The owners felt that the change was needed particularly after
the national pastime's image had been sullied by the Black
Sox Scandal of 1920. They were proved right, as offensive
statistics and attendance figures reached unprecedented
highs in the 1920s. Also JACKRABBIT BALL and KANGA-
ROO BALL. (It should be noted that the rabbit ball and high-
scoring baseball have always had their detractors. One of
them was short story writer and former baseball scribe Ring
Lardner, who lamented the death of old-style "inside baseball" and derided the lively new ball as the "Br'er Rabbit Ball"
and the "TNT ball.")

radio ball: n. A pitch thrown with such velocity that the batter claims he could only hear the ball and not see it. Catfish
Metkovich, a Pittsburgh Pirate outfielder–first baseman during the early 1950s, is credited with coining "radio ball" after

RABBIT

striking out on a blazing fastball from Boston Brave pitcher Max Surkont.

rainbow: n. 1. A high arcing fly ball, especially a home run. 2. A high arcing curve ball.

rain check: n. The detachable part of an admission ticket, which, in the event that a game is postponed because of inclement weather, the bearer can use for admission to the replaying of the game. Rain checks were first used in New Orleans in 1889, when baseball club owner Abner Powell devised the concept. Previously, whenever a game had been rained out, ticket-holders had to buy new tickets to the replayed game. Powell thought this unfair and came up with the rain check.

rain delay: n. The temporary halting of play because of rain.

rainmaker: n. A fly ball with such a high arc that it seemingly could punch a hole in the clouds and let loose a torrent of rain.

rain-out: n. Postponement or cancellation of a game because of rain.

rally: n. An outburst of hits and runs by the batting team in an inning.
    v. To make a rally.

range: n. A fielder's, particularly an infielder's, ability to reach batted balls by moving to his right or his left. A fielder who can cut off balls well away from his original fielding position has "good range" or "a lot of range."

Rawlings lobotomy: n. A pitch that hits a batter in the head. Rawlings is a company that manufactures baseballs. Also BEAN BALL and BEANER.

RBI: n. 1. A run batted in. 2. The abbreviation for "run batted in."

receiver: n. The catcher, who "receives" the pitches.

regulation game: n. A game in which the losing side has had at least five team at bats. In that case, a game may be halted at any subsequent point for such reasons as inclement weather or darkness and be an official and complete game.

relay: n. A throw by one fielder to another, who then throws the ball to yet another fielder in an attempt to put out a baserunner. The most common type of relay occurs when an outfielder plays a batted ball off the outfield wall and throws the ball to an infielder, who in turn throws the ball to the catcher in an effort to tag out a runner at home plate.

release: n. The act of letting go of the ball while throwing it. This word most frequently applies to the manner in which a pitcher lets go of, or "releases," the ball.

relief: n. The replacing of one player by another player during a game, especially one pitcher substituting for another.
      adj. Of or relating to relief, particularly in regard to bullpen pitchers.

relief ace: n. A team's best relief pitcher. Also BULLPEN ACE. See ACE.

reliefer, relief pitcher, reliever: n. A pitcher whose primary role is to come into a game to replace another pitcher. The relief pitcher did not become a major force in big league baseball until the 1920s, when Wilcy Moore of the New York Yankees and Firpo Marberry of the Washington Senators became the first hurlers to work primarily in relief. James Otis "Doc" or "Otey" Crandall, who came up with the New York Giants in 1908, reportedly was the first pitcher to be hired expressly for relief. See LONG MAN, SAVE, and SHORT RELIEVER.

reserve: n. A player who is not in the starting lineup, either for a particular game or on a regular basis. The reserve player's duties include pinch-hitting, pinch-running, and replacing a defensive player.

reserve clause: n. A clause once included in baseball contracts, which bound the player permanently to his team until the management sold, traded, or released him. This controversial clause, which had been upheld by a United States Supreme Court ruling in 1922 and in effect granted professional baseball exemption from antitrust laws, was challenged in 1970 by a National League outfielder named Curt Flood. After being traded in 1969 from the St. Louis Cardinals to the Philadelphia Phillies, Flood challenged the reserve clause, claiming that he should have the right to sell his services without being controlled by the whim of the team with which he signed his first pro contract. The Supreme Court denied his challenge in 1971, ruling again that baseball was exempt from antitrust laws. But the beginning of the end of the reserve clause was drawing near. In late 1974 arbitrator Peter M. Seitz ruled that Oakland A's pitcher Jim "Catfish" Hunter was no longer bound to the club because of a technicality in his contract. Hunter promptly declared himself a free agent and was signed by the New York Yankees for $3.25 million. A year later, Seitz decided that pitchers Andy Messersmith of the Los Angeles Dodgers and Dave McNally of the Montreal Expos were no longer bound to their teams and could become free agents because their clubs had agreed to let them pitch the previous season without being signed. Thus, Seitz said, the two pitchers were free to place themselves on the open market. A federal court later upheld Seitz's ruling. The reserve clause had struck out, and the custom of spending exorbitant sums of money on free agents had begun, for better or worse.

resin bag: See ROSIN BAG.

resin ball: n. A ball that has been rubbed or dabbed with resin powder to make it break sharply when pitched. The resin ball was one of the pitches outlawed by baseball in 1920.

retire: v. To put out, as in "Seaver retires Rose on a fly ball to the right fielder."

retire the side: v. To put out the offensive team in an inning.

reverse curve: n. A screwball, which breaks opposite to the way a regular curve ball breaks. For example, when a right-handed pitcher throws a curve ball, it breaks to his left, but when he throws a screwball, it breaks to his right. See SCREW-BALL.

rhubarb: n. A heated dispute on the field during a game. Red Barber, the renowned radio broadcaster for the Brooklyn Dodgers, popularized "rhubarb." Barber picked it up from a sportswriter friend of his, Garry Schumacher, who had heard it from another sportswriter, Tom Meany, who had himself gotten the expression from a Brooklyn bartender. As Barber tells it, Meany went into a Brooklyn saloon one day after a shooting had occurred there. The bartender told Meany that the bar had seen quite a "rhubarb," and later explained that he had used that word because a bowl of rhubarb had always struck him as a particularly messy sight.

rib, ribbie: n. A run batted in. The words derive from the abbreviation for "run batted in" (RBI).

rifle: n. A strong throwing arm. Also BAZOOKA, CANNON, and GUN.
    v. To make a strong and accurate throw.

right, right field: n. 1. The area of the outfield between center field and the right field foul line. 2. The position played by the right fielder. 3. A nickname for the right fielder.

right fielder: n. The defensive player positioned in right field. Also RIGHT and RIGHT FIELD.

rising fastball: n. A fastball that rises as it nears home plate, often eluding the batter's swing. Also UPSHOOT.

road trip: n. One or more series of games played in the opponents' home ballparks. The first baseball road trip on record was undertaken by the amateur Brooklyn Excelsiors, whose three-game journey to Albany, Troy, and Buffalo, New York, began on June 30, 1860, and ended in an Excelsior sweep.

rock: n. 1. The part of a pitcher's throwing motion in which he steps backward. 2. The baseball.
    v. To step backward during a pitching motion.

rocket: n. A sharply hit line drive.

role player: n. A reserve player, a nonstarter. This term became popular in the 1970s and is essentially a euphemism for "benchwarmer" or "reserve." A player feels more valuable when he can say that he's "filling a role" rather than "warming the bench." Even baseball is not immune to the modern age of specialization and its fuzzy jargon.

roller: n. A ground ball that rolls at slow to moderate speed.

rook, rookie: n. A first-year player. There are two possible origins of the word. One theory holds that "rookie" comes from Army slang for a new soldier or a "recruit." The other theory states that "rookie" derives from the chess piece called the rook, which, like a young player on a ball team, must wait to be played until all the other "pieces" have been moved. Also DONKEY, IVORY, YAN, and YANNIGAN.

Rookie of the Year Award: n. An annual award recognizing the best rookie player in both the American and National Leagues. Introduced in 1947, the award was given to only one player in the major leagues until 1949, the year the awards began being presented to the top first-year men from each league. Jackie Robinson, who broke major league baseball's color line by joining the Brooklyn Dodgers in 1947, won the first Rookie of the Year Award. He hit .297, led the league with 29 stolen bases, and helped Brooklyn win the NL pennant. In 1975 Boston Red Sox outfielder Fred Lynn became the first man to win awards as both Rookie of the Year and Most Valuable Player in the same season. His .331 average, 21 home runs, and 105 runs batted in contributed greatly to Boston's American League pennant. The Rookie of the Year Award is decided by a vote among the members of the Baseball Writers Association of America.

root: v. To support and be a fan of a particular team. The word dates to the late 1800s, when it was observed that fans were "rooted" to their favorite teams. Subsequently, fans also became known as "rooters."

rooter: n. A fan. See ROOT.

rope: n. A sharply hit line drive, a shortened version of the expression "frozen rope."

rosin bag: n. A small bag made of mesh and filled with powdered rosin. During a game, a pitcher can put rosin on his throwing hand to better grip the ball. The rosin bag is kept on the pitcher's mound, but when introduced to the major leagues in 1925, rosin bags were carried by umpires and supplied to the pitchers upon request. Also RESIN BAG.

rotation: n. 1. A team's regular starting pitchers, who work on a "rotation" basis of one start usually every four or five days. 2. The spin on a batted or thrown ball.

round: n. An inning. The term is borrowed from the sport of boxing.

roundhouse: n. A curve ball thrown with a sidearm delivery. The term derives from the curved buildings in which locomotives are housed and repaired.

round-tripper: n. A home run, during which a player makes a "round trip" starting and finishing at home plate.

route-going performance: n. A game in which the starting pitcher works every inning for his team, or "goes the route." Also COMPLETE GAME.

rubber: See PITCHER'S RUBBER.

rubber arm: n. A durable pitcher, one whose throwing arm escapes the injuries that plague most hurlers. Also IRON MAN.

run: n. A point scored when a baserunner safely crosses home plate. The word was borrowed from cricket. The object of baseball is, of course, to score more runs than the opposing team.
    v. See EJECT.

run and hit: n. A play in which the runner on first base starts to second base on the pitch, while the batter has the option of swinging at the pitch or not. The batter swings with the intention of getting a base hit that would allow the runner to advance to third base or even score. Even if the batter should hit an infield ground ball, the defense would have little or no time to put out the runner at second base, and so he probably would be advanced. If the batter does not swing, then the runner slides into second base on an attempted steal. Compare HIT AND RUN.
    v. To do a run and hit.

run batted in: n. A run that has scored as the result of an action by the batter. A batter can drive in a run in the following ways: by getting a base hit that scores one or more of the runners on base, by getting a base on balls or being hit by a pitch with the bases loaded, by making a sacrifice or a sacrifice fly, or by reaching on an error with less than two outs on a play that would have scored a runner from third base even if the error had not been committed. Abbreviated RBI. Also RIB and RIBBIE. Introduction by a Buffalo newspaper in 1879, the RBI became an official major league statistic in 1920.

run down: v. To put out a baserunner in a rundown. See RUNDOWN.

rundown: n. A play in which a baserunner is caught, or "hung up," between two bases while the defensive team attempts to tag him out. Also PICKLE.

run out a hit: v. To run at full speed after hitting a ball. A batter runs out a hit in the hope that the defense will make an error on a routinely easy play such as an infield ground ball or a pop fly.

runner: See BASERUNNER.

runners at the corners: n. Baserunners at first base and third base, the two bases often referred to as a baseball diamond's "corners."

rush seat: n. An unreserved seat at a ballpark, usually a bleacher seat. During baseball's early days, when ballparks were small structures that had far fewer seats than the big stadiums of today, the gates would be opened and customers would "rush" in to grab the best unreserved seats.

sabermetrics: n.The mathematical study of baseball records. Named for the acronym of the Society for American Baseball Research (SABR), which was formed in 1971, sabermetrics attempts to uncover some of the game's hidden points and challenge much of its traditional wisdom, often by devising new statistics such as Bill James's Range Factor and Runs Created and Thomas Boswell's Total Average. While the word "sabermetrics" is new and the field has been burgeoning since SABR's founding, baseball observers have been studying records and inventing new statistics since as early as the mid-1800s.

sack: See BASE.

sacker: n. An infielder, specifically one whose position is named after one of the bases, or "sacks"—a first, second, or third baseman.

sacrifice: n. A play in which the batter makes an out while enabling a baserunner or baserunners to advance, thus "sacrificing" himself for the good of the team. Also SACRIFICE HIT. See SACRIFICE BUNT and SACRIFICE FLY.
    v. To make a sacrifice.

sacrifice bunt: n. A bunt that causes the batter to be put out at first base but enables a baserunner or baserunners to advance. A batter who makes a sacrifice bunt is not charged with a time at bat.

sacrifice fly: n. A fly ball that is caught and enables a runner to tag up and score from third base. A batter who hits a sacrifice fly is not charged with a time at bat. In 1908 the rule was established in its present form, thanks to a protest to National League officials by Philadelphia Phillies manager Billy Murray. One of Murray's players, outfielder Sherry Magee, often hit long fly balls that would score men from third base. Murray argued that it was unfair to charge Magee with making outs when, in fact, he was helping the team with his long flies. The rule was instated, and then expanded in 1926 so that a fly enabling any baserunner to advance was classified as a sacrifice fly. In 1939 the rule was completely abandoned, but in 1954 it was restored to the 1908 version.

sacrifice hit: See SACRIFICE (n.).

safety: See BASE HIT.

safety squeeze: See SQUEEZE PLAY.

sandpaper ball: n. A ball that has been illegally defaced by being partly rubbed with sandpaper, which would cause the ball to break sharply when thrown by the pitcher.

save: n. A credit given to a relief pitcher who finishes a game won by his team. He must have entered the game with a lead of no more than three runs and pitched at least one inning, or entered the game with the potential tying run on base, at bat or on deck, or pitched effectively for at least three innings. The save was officially adopted by the major leagues in 1969 and was baseball's first new stat in nearly 50 years. Chicago sportswriter Jerome Holtzman gets credit for being the main advocate of the save, having long used his newspaper columns to promote the stat's official adoption. Also VULTCH. Compare HOLD and SQUANDER.

saw off: v. To pitch inside to a batter, especially toward his hands. When the batter swings at such a pitch, he can hit only weakly off the bat handle. The pitcher has "sawed off" the bat.

"Say it ain't so, Joe!": See BLACK SOX SCANDAL.

scatter-armed: adj. Wild, having no control. The term is most often applied to a pitcher whose deliveries wind up everywhere except in the strike zone. Also ALL OVER THE PLATE and WILD.

scientific baseball: See INSIDE BASEBALL.

score: n. A run, a point earned when a runner safely crosses home plate.
    v. 1. To cross home plate safely and make a run. 2. To keep a record of a ball game on a scorecard. See SCORE-CARD. 3. To serve as official scorer of a ball game. See OFFI-CIAL SCORER.

scorecard: n. A sheet of paper, often included in programs sold at ballparks, on which one can record the batter-by-batter progress of a game. The first scorecards date to the 1880s when they were sold by Ed Barrow and Harry Stevens at the ballpark of a minor league team in Wheeling, West Virginia. Barrow later became the manager of the Boston Red Sox and the general manager of the New York Yankees, while Stevens became a renowned baseball concessions magnate. He would become a multimillionaire on his scorecard business alone. Also PROGRAM.

scoring position: n. A point from which a baserunner can easily score on a base hit (second or third base) or a sacrifice (third base).

scout: n. 1. A full-time or part-time employee of a team who hunts down talented young prospects in the hope of signing them to a contract with his team. Also BIRD DOG and IVORY HUNTER. 2. A defensive player who, in the days before Alexander Cartwright wrote the basic rules of modern baseball in 1845, positioned himself behind the catcher and caught and made plays on wild pitches, passed balls, and any batted ball. Like a cricket field, a baseball field of that era had no foul territory. Therefore, any kind of batted ball was in play.

v. To seek out and note the progress of a young baseball prospect, while in the employ of a team that's interested in signing the prospect to a contract.

scratch hit: n. A base hit on which the batter barely made contact, or just "scratched," the ball. Such a hit rolls slowly on the infield grass and allows the batter to reach first base before a play can be made on him. Also INFIELD HIT.

screamer, screaming meemie: n. An extremely fast line drive. The term is said to have been originally applied to German rocket shells during World War II and later adapted to baseball.

screwball: n. A slow curve ball that breaks opposite to the way a curve breaks. For example, when a right-handed pitcher throws a normal curve, the ball breaks to his left. But when he throws a screwball, it breaks to his right. Christy Mathewson, the great New York Giant pitcher of the early 1900s, threw the first version of the screwball, known as the "fadeaway." About 1930, another Giant pitcher, Carl Hubbell, made the screwball famous by making it his primary pitch and winning big with it. Also REVERSE CURVE and SCROOGIE. See TURN THE BALL OVER.

scroogie: n. A nickname for the screwball. The word originated about 1960. See SCREWBALL.

scrub, scrubeenie: n. A reserve player, one whose playing time comes usually during the late innings of a game that has virtually been decided. He replaces, or "scrubs up" for, starting players.

scuffball, scuffer: n. A ball that has been illegally scuffed or defaced in such a way as to cause it to curve when thrown by the pitcher. Also EMERY BALL.

seagull: n. A weakly hit fly ball that drops quickly, somewhat like a swooping seagull. Of the same species as the DYING QUAIL.

season ticket: n. A ticket program offered by baseball clubs, in which the customer can buy the same stadium seat or seats for all or many of the home games in a season. The season ticket was developed in 1884 by the National League franchise in Providence, Rhode Island. If purchased before March 15, the Providence fan had to pay only $15 for a season ticket. If purchased after April 15, he had to fork over $20.

second, second base: n. 1. The base set at the top corner of the baseball diamond, on a straight line with the pitcher's mound and home plate. Also KEYSTONE. 2. The position played by the second baseman. 3. A nickname for the second baseman.

second baseman: n. The defensive player generally positioned halfway between first base and second base in the infield.

seed: n. A baseball, particularly a ball thrown or batted with such velocity that it seems as small as a seed.

seeing-eye hit: See BALL HAD EYES, THE.

send the runner or runners: v. To signal to the baserunner or baserunners to start running on the next pitch, as part of a steal attempt, a hit and run, or a run and hit.

senior circuit: n. The National League, so called because it is the older of the two current major leagues. The National League was founded in 1876, the American League, or the "junior circuit," in 1901. See also NATIONAL LEAGUE.

series: n. A set of two or more games between two teams. A team's regular season schedule consists of series with the other teams in its league. Also SET.

Series, The: n. A shortened name for the World Series.

set: n. 1. A series of games between two teams. Also SERIES. 2. The point of a pitcher's delivery when, while pitching from the stretch, he rests his hands on his belt buckle. The pitcher must make a set during his motion or he will be called by the umpire for committing a balk. Also SET POSITION. See STRETCH. Compare WINDUP (n.).
  v. To come to a set position during a pitching delivery from the stretch.

set down: v. To put out a team in an inning without allowing any of the three batters to reach base. Also MOW DOWN and SKUNK. See ONE-TWO-THREE and THREE UP, THREE DOWN.

set position: See SET.

setup man: See LONG MAN, LONG RELIEVER.

seven o'clock hitter: See ONE O'CLOCK HITTER.

seventh-inning stretch: n. A traditional custom at baseball games, in which customers stand and stretch before the bottom half of the seventh inning. The origin of the seventh-inning stretch is uncertain, but three theories exist. The first claims that Cincinnati Redleg fans stood during the seventh frame of a game in 1869 to alleviate the discomfort of sitting on the ballpark's hard wooden benches. (Some things never change.) The second theory holds that students at Manhattan College stood up to cool off during the seventh inning of a college contest played on a hot afternoon in 1882. The third theory is the best-known of the three. The story goes that President William Howard Taft, while attending a season home opener in Washington in 1910, rose and stretched during the seventh inning. Thinking the president was leaving, the patrons in the ballpark stood up out of respect. That game also saw the beginning of another baseball tradition, the throwing out of the first ball by a U.S. president. See THROW OUT THE FIRST BALL.

shade: v. To position oneself on the side of the field toward which the batter is expected to hit the ball. Compare SHIFT and STRAIGHT AWAY.

shag flies: v. To practice catching fly balls. Players usually shag flies in practice sessions before games.

shake off a sign: v. While pitching, to disagree with a catcher's signal and ask for a new signal by shaking the head. For example, a catcher might signal a pitcher to throw a curve. The pitcher wants to throw a fastball and "shakes off" the curve signal.

shave the corners: v. To throw pitches consistently over the corners of the plate for strikes. Also PAINT THE BLACK.

shell: v. To get many hits, particularly extra base hits, against a pitcher and his team. The word stems from military jargon for bombing a site with rocket shells.

shift: n. A defensive alignment in which the fielders, especially the infielders, position themselves on the side of the field toward which the batter is expected to hit the ball. "Shifting" is more exaggerated a move than "shading" a batter, and is rarely done, usually only when a powerful pull hitter is batting. One of the most famous shifts was the one used against Ted Williams, the great left-handed slugger of the Boston Red Sox. With Williams at bat, many teams brought their shortstop over to play behind second base, expecting Williams to pull the ball. If he did pull the ball toward the right side of the infield, the first baseman, the second baseman, or the shortstop would have little trouble getting to the ball. Williams refused to slap hits to the left side of the field and still finished his career with a .344 lifetime batting average. Compare SHADE and STRAIGHT AWAY.

   v. To align the defense in a shift.

shine ball: n. A ball that has been illegally tampered with to make it smoother and shinier on one side than on the other. The ball's uneven surface causes it to do funny things in the air currents, one of which is to veer unexpectedly as the pitch nears home plate. Over the years pitchers have "shined" up balls with materials ranging from saliva to hair tonic to vaginal cream. In the early 1900s, when baseballs were rarely replaced during games, batters had to contend with the shine ball's discoloration as well as its troublesome movement. See DOCTORED BALL.

shin guards: n. Protective plastic-covered pads that the catcher wears on his shins. The first shin guards were invented and worn in 1908 by New York Giant catcher Roger Bresnahan, who is also credited with devising the batting helmet.

shoes: During baseball's early days, players wore shoes with cleated soles. The Harvard College ball club allegedly introduced leather shoes in the late 1870s. Metal spikes were not common until about 1890, and immediately players found that they enjoyed better footing at bat, on the basepaths, and in the field with their spiked shoes. In that rougher era of the sport, players often tried to intimidate their opponents by sitting on the field before a game and silently filing their spikes until they were dangerously sharp. Infielders certainly got the point when enemy players slid into them spikes-first. Now players have two types of shoe—the traditional spiked model for games on grass, and a rubber-soled shoe for play on artificial surfaces. Another significant change in baseball shoes over the years has been the shift from the all-black shoe to shoes of various colors and decorative designs. Because of their soles, baseball shoes are sometimes referred to as "cleats" and "spikes."

shoestring catch: n. A catch that the fielder makes by gloving the ball just above his shoestrings and usually after running a long distance at full speed. Most shoestring catches are made on balls hit to the outfield.

short: n. 1. The area of the infield in which the shortstop plays. 2. The defensive position played by the shortstop. 3. A nickname for the shortstop.

short hop: See IN-BETWEEN HOP.

short-hop: v. To field a ball immediately after it bounces on the ground, or on the "short hop" or "in-between hop."

short man, short reliever: n. A relief pitcher who specializes in entering games when the outcome is on the line. He usually works about three innings or less, a situation known as "short relief." Some of the best "short men" of recent years include Goose Gossage, Rollie Fingers, Bruce Sutter, and Dan Quisenberry. Compare LONG MAN, LONG RELIEVER.

short porch: n. The seating area of a ballpark, just beyond either the right field or left field wall and near either foul pole, which is a relatively short distance from home plate. Short porches such as the ones down the right field line at New York's Yankee Stadium and Boston's Fenway Park have accounted for many easy home runs over the years.

shortstop: n. 1. The defensive player who generally is positioned halfway between second base and third base and farther back on the infield dirt than any of the other three infielders. 2. The area of the field in which the shortstop plays. 3. The defensive position played by the shortstop. 4. A nickname for the shortstop. Also SHORT (for all four definitions).

shut out: v. To pitch a shutout, to hold the opposing team scoreless. Also BLANK, CHICAGO, and WHITEWASH.

shutout: n. A game in which one team is held scoreless by the other team. During the 1870s, a shutout was known as a "Chicago" because Chicago's National League club often held their opponents scoreless. In 1879 a writer in Troy, New York became the first scribe to apply the term "shutout" to baseball. He borrowed it from the sport of horse racing, in which "shutout" means unable to place a bet because the race has begun. Also CHICAGO, KALSOMINE, and WHITEWASH.

sidearm: adj. Relating to a pitch or a throw that a player makes by bringing his throwing arm across his body.
    adv. With a sidearm manner.
    v. To make a pitch or a throw with a sidearm motion.

sign, signal: n. An instruction made verbally or with a gesture from a player, coach, or manager to a player on the field.
    v. To make a sign or signal.

single: n. A base hit on which the batter reaches and stops at first base. Also BINGLE and SINGLETON.
    v. To make a single.

singleton: See SINGLE.

sinker, sinker ball, sinker pitch: n. A pitch, generally not a curve ball, that drops suddenly as it nears home plate.

sit on a pitch: v. To wait for a specific pitch during an at bat, one that the batter feels he can hit well.

sitting in the catbird seat: adv. phrase. In an advantageous position. The phrase was popularized by Red Barber when he broadcast Brooklyn Dodger games during the 1940s and 1950s. Writer James Thurber used "The Catbird Seat" as the title of his short story about a woman who drove a male coworker crazy with her continuous use of such Barberisms as "sitting in the catbird seat" and "tearing up the pea patch." Barber himself has said he is uncertain of the expression's exact origin, although he has said that he picked it up in a game of stud poker. Barber held two 8's and kept raising the pot, and finally lost to a friend who was holding two aces. Raking in his winnings, the friend said to Barber, "Thanks for all those raises. From the start I was sitting in the catbird seat."

skip, skipper: n. The field manager of a baseball team. See MANAGER.

skunk: v. To put out a team in an inning by retiring the first three batters who come to bat. The word dates from the late 1800s. Also MOW DOWN and SET DOWN. See ONE-TWO-THREE and THREE UP, THREE DOWN.

sky: v. To hit an especially high fly ball.

slab: See PITCHER'S RUBBER.

slab artist, slabber, slabbist: n. A pitcher, who works with one foot on the pitching rubber, also known as the "slab."

slant: n. A curve ball, which "slants" on its way to home plate.

slap hit: n. A base hit that the batter makes by extending his bat, or "slapping," at a pitch on the outside part of the plate. A batter who often makes this type of hit is called a "slap hitter," a label that suggests he has little power.

sleeper rabbit play: n. A set baserunning play attempted with runners on second and third bases. The runner on second tries to draw a throw from the catcher by returning slowly to his base after a pitch. If the catcher does throw to second, each runner breaks toward the next base. The play was invented in the early 1900s by George Moriarty while he was a first baseman-third baseman for the Detroit Tigers.

slice: v. To hit a ball that curves sharply away from the side of the field on which the batter is standing. For instance, a right-handed batter would "slice" a ball to right field.

slide: v. To dive feet-first or head-first while approaching a base so as to arrive more quickly or to elude the fielder's tag.
n. The act of sliding into a base. See CHICAGO SLIDE and POP-UP SLIDE.

slider: n. A pitch that is thrown with a fastball motion and travels like a fastball until it makes a small but sudden curve as it nears home plate. Also NICKLE CURVE, a derisive term for what many batters consider to be a second-rate curve ball. The slider is traced to Brooklyn's Elmer Stricklett, who is said to have brought the pitch to the big leagues in 1904. Some historians claim that the pitch was probably thrown, if not named, well before that date. However, it was not until the early 1960s that the slider became an oft-used pitch, supposedly because the lesser talents who were elevated to major league status after expansion needed an extra pitch, something other than their second-rate fastballs and curves, to get out batters.

sliding pit: n. The dirt areas around each base and home plate on artificial-turf fields. The "pits" were installed to spare the players from having to slide on the rock-hard fake turf.

slip pitch: n. A slow breaking pitch thrown by letting the ball "slip" out of the pitcher's hand. The ball is gripped between the thumb and the palm.

slop: See JUNK.

slugfest: n. A game in which both teams make many base hits and runs. The greatest slugfest in a single game occurred on August 24, 1922, when the Chicago Cubs beat the Philadelphia Phillies 26–23. (The Cubs, incidentally, were leading 25–4 after four innings, and managed to withstand a 19-run explosion by the Phils.)

slugger: n. A powerful batter, one who tends to make many extra base hits, especially home runs. Babe Ruth is the archetypal slugger, though Boston's Charley Jones is credited with being baseball's first power hitter for his 9 home runs and 62 runs batted in during 1879.

slugging average, slugging percentage: n. The statistical average that measures a batter's frequency of making extra base hits. To figure a player's slugging average, divide his total bases (the bases he achieved by reaching safely on base hits) by his total times at bat. Henry Chadwick, the baseball reporter and statistician of the 1800s, devised in the 1860s a primitive version of the slugging average called "total bases average," which tabulated bases per game rather than bases per at bat. Slugging average was not accepted as an official stat until 1923 by the National League and 1946 by the American League.

slump: n. A lengthy period of time during which a player or a team performs poorly, at bat, in the field, or on the mound.
     v. To be in a slump.

slurve: n. A pitch that is a cross between a slider and a curve. It moves faster than a curve but breaks more than a slider.

smoke: n. A fastball or many fastballs.
     v. 1. To throw a ball with great velocity. 2. To hit a ball very hard.

smoke the batter: v. To throw many fastballs to a batter, particularly toward the inside part of the plate.

smother in leather: v. To make many outstanding defensive plays that prevent the opposing team from putting together enough hits to score any runs. "Leather" refers to the defensive team's gloves.

snake: n. A curve ball, which is as tortuous (and, many batters would say, as dangerous) as a snake.

sneaky-fast, sneaky-quick: adj. Faster than one assumes. These expressions refer to a pitcher who, because of some mechanical aspect of his delivery or the way he mixes up his pitches, throws a fastball that's speedier than the batter expects.

snow cone: See ICE CREAM CONE.

soft hands: n. The hands of a fielder who rarely misplays a ball. The ball seems to go so gently and willingly into his glove that he is said to possess "soft hands." Compare CLANG, HARD HANDS, and IRON HANDS.

solo home run, solo shot: n. A home run with no one on base.

soupbone: n. A pitcher's arm. The word dates from the early 1900s, as does "soupboning," which means "pitching."

southpaw: n. A player, particularly a pitcher, who throws with his left arm. The word allegedly was coined in 1887 by *Chicago News* sportswriter Finley Peter Dunne. In baseball's early days, most ballparks were laid out with home plate on the west side of the field. Thus, the throwing arm of a left-handed pitcher would be on the field's south side. (So how come right-handed pitchers aren't called "northpaws"?) Also LEFTY and PORTSIDER.

Spanish baseball terms: The United States is almost matched in its quality of baseball players and fervor of baseball fans by the athletes and rooters of Spanish-speaking countries, such as Mexico, Cuba, and the nations of Central America and South America. President Fidel Castro of Cuba is said to have aspired to play in the major leagues. It's been said that had he shown a little more ability, Cuba might not be a Communist country today. At any rate, baseball translates into Spanish, and some examples are given below (see FRENCH BASE-BALL TERMS):

baseball (the ball) = "pelota"
baseball (the game) = "beisbol"
base hit = "bola bateada con exito"
bat = "bate"
batter = "bateador"
catcher = "cacher," "receptor," "parador"
doubleheader = "doble encuentro"
hit a fly ball = "pegar una planchita," "elevar una palo-
         mita"
home run = "jonron"
pinch hitter = "bateador sustituto"
pitcher = "lanzador," "tirador"
rhubarb = "barahunda"

spear: v. To lunge at and catch a sharply hit ball. Also STAB.

speedball: n. A fastball.

speed merchant: n. A fast runner, so fast that he has speed to sell. Also RABBIT.

spike: v. To slide toward a fielder at a base and cut him, either intentionally or accidentally, with the spikes on the bottom of the baserunner's shoes.

spikes: See SHOES.

spin the batter's cap: v. To throw a pitch at a batter, usually deliberately, causing him to "spin his cap," or turn away quickly to avoid being hit by the ball. See BRUSH BACK.

spitball, spitter: n. A ball that has been illegally dabbed with saliva or other substances ranging from hair cream to vaginal cream to powdered rosin to pine tar, to make the ball break sharply and unexpectedly when pitched to a batter. The spitball reportedly was invented in 1902 by George Hildebrand, an outfielder for a minor league team in Providence, and like many great inventions, the spitter came about accidentally. While playing catch before a game with rookie pitcher Frank Corridon, Hildebrand inadvertently put some saliva on the ball. He threw it and both he and Corridon noticed the severe dip the ball took. Corridon decided to try the trick on the mound, and used it to some success. The spitball and other doctored pitches were banned from major league baseball in 1920, although a "grandfather clause" allowed each team to carry as many as two pitchers who were already known practitioners of the slippery pitch. The 17 hurlers covered under the grandfather clause were American Leaguers Doc Ayers, Ray Caldwell, Stanley Coveleski, Red Faber, Dutch Leonard, John Picus Quinn, Allen Russell, Urban Shocker, and Allen Sothoron, and National Leaguers Bill Doak, Phil Douglas, Dana Fillingim, Ray Fisher, Marvin Goodwin, Burleigh Grimes, Clarence Mitchell, and Dick Rudolph. Also CUBAN FORK BALL, DROOLER, and STATEN ISLAND SINKER. See DOCTORED BALL.

split: v. To win and lose an equal number of games in a doubleheader or a series.

n. The result of two teams "splitting" a doubleheader or a series.

split-fingered fastball: n. A pitch gripped with the index and middle fingers spread wide over the ball and thrown with the motion used to deliver a fastball. The result is a pitch that suddenly sinks as it nears home plate, like a spitball, only without the spit. Roger Craig is credited with inventing the pitch, and won wide acclaim for teaching it to the Detroit Tiger pitching staff, which he coached, during the early 1980s. Bruce Sutter and later Detroit's Jack Morris were the first masters of the split-fingered fastball, also known as "The Pitch of the 1980s."

spot: adj. Occasional. For example, a pitcher who starts games only occasionally is referred to as a "spot" starter.

spray hitter: n. A batter who tends to hit, or "spray," the ball to all parts of the field.

spring training: n. The five-to-eight-week period before the start of the regular season, when major league teams hold training camps in various sites in Florida, Arizona, and California. The first spring training trip was taken in 1884 by the Boston Nationals, who encamped in New Orleans. Over the years teams have held spring training in states all around the south and southwest, and even farther north during World War II. During the last four decades, the clubs have become firmly entrenched in the three states mentioned above. See CACTUS LEAGUE, GRAPEFRUIT LEAGUE, and LANDIS LINE.

squander: n. A statistic that keeps track of each time a relief pitcher enters a game with his team leading or tied and leaves the game with his team trailing. Major league teams began tabulating this still unofficial stat around 1980. Compare HOLD and SAVE.

square: n. Home plate, which was a 12-inch square until 1900, when it was changed to its modern five-sided, 17-inch-wide shape.

square around: v. To turn from one's regular batting stance and face the pitcher so as to bunt the pitched ball.

square stance: See PARALLEL STANCE.

squeeze: n. A squeeze play.
    v. To make a squeeze play. See SQUEEZE PLAY.

squeeze play: n. An arranged play in which the runner on third base takes off for home plate while the batter attempts to bunt the ball and thus enable the runner to cross the plate before a play can be made on him. When the runner waits for the batter to bunt the ball and then starts toward the plate, the play is called a "safety squeeze." It is a "suicide squeeze" when the runner starts toward the plate as the pitcher releases the ball, not waiting to see if the batter makes contact with the pitch.

squib: v. To hit a squibber. See SQUIBBER.

squibber: n. A weakly hit ball that usually does not roll or fly past the infield. Such a hit packs as much pop as a "squib," a dud firecracker.

stab: n. A fielder's lunging stop of a batted ball.
v. To make a stab. Also SPEAR.

standings: n. The order of teams in a league or a division, according to their wins and losses.

stand-up hit: n. A base hit—a double, triple, or home run—in which the batter arrives safely and standing at the base, not having to slide.

stand-up slide: See POP-UP SLIDE.

stanza: n. An inning, which is a section of a baseball game, just as a stanza is a section of a poem.

start: v. To play as a member of the starting lineup.
n. The act of playing in the starting lineup. The term, in both noun and verb forms, is most often applied to pitchers.

starting lineup: n. The players who are in the lineup at the start of the game.

starting pitcher: n. The pitcher in the starting lineup.

Staten Island sinker: n. A euphemistic term for a spitball. The expression is often attributed to George Bamberger, a pitching coach for the Baltimore Orioles during the late 1960s and early 1970s and later a manager for the Milwaukee Brewers and the New York Mets, and a native of Staten Island, New York.

Statue of Liberty: n. A player who takes a third strike, so called because he stands as motionless as the lady with the lamp. Such a player is also said to be doing a "statue stunt." Also WOODEN INDIAN.

steal: n. A play in which a baserunner starts running for the next base and arrives before he can be tagged out. The most common type of steal occurs when the runner starts running just before the pitcher releases the ball toward home plate and arrives at the next base before the catcher can throw the ball to the fielder covering the bag that the runner is attempting to steal. Also STOLEN BASE. See DELAYED DOUBLE STEAL, DOUBLE STEAL, SLEEPER RABBIT PLAY, and TRIPLE STEAL.

    v. To steal a base.

steam: n. A fastball or many fastballs.

Stengelese: n. The fractured and often comical brand of English spoken by Charles Dillon "Casey" Stengel. His major league experience included 14 years as a player and 25 as a manager, most notably as the skipper of the New York Yankees from 1949 to 1960. During that stretch the Yanks won ten pennants and seven World Series. Stengel—or "The Old Perfessor," as he was called—was as renowned for his comical way with words as for his managerial skills. Some examples of Stengelese:

- In comparing two players, Casey remarked, "They're alike in a lot of similarities."
- During a conversation with a reporter, Stengel said, "I won't trade my left fielder." The writer asked, "Who is

your left fielder?" "I don't know," said Casey, "but if it isn't him, I'll keep him anyway."

- At the age of 70, Casey was fired by the Yankees, ostensibly because of his age. "Most people my age are dead," he sagely noted, and then added his trademark line—
- "You can look it up."

step in the bucket: See FOOT IN THE BUCKET.

stick: n. 1. A bat. 2. A batter, as in "This team has a lot of good sticks."

stick the ball in the batter's ear: v. To throw a pitch at the batter's head, without actually hitting him. To do this, the pitcher must first be angry about something that occurred earlier in the game. After the pitch, the batter is in none too cheery a mood either. See BRUSH BACK.

sting: n. A base hit. The word dates back to the early 1900s.

stolen base: See STEAL.

stopper: n. A pitcher, usually a starter, who has a reputation for "stopping" losing streaks by his team or "stopping" key opponents in crucial games. The term also may refer to a relief pitcher who is often called on to squelch a lead-threatening rally late in a game. See CORK.

straight away: adj. In a normal defensive position. When the defense is said to be playing a batter "straight away," that means the fielders are standing in their usual defensive spots, not shifted in expectation of the batter's pulling or slapping the ball in a definite direction. Compare SHADE and SHIFT.

straight change: See CHANGE, CHANGE OF PACE, and CHANGE-UP.

straight stance: See PARALLEL STANCE.

straight steal: n. A steal that is not part of another play, such as a hit and run or a run and hit.

strand: v. To leave runners on base at the end of an inning. See LEFT ON BASE.

stretch: n. One of the two pitching motions, the other being the windup. In the stretch, the pitcher places the exterior side of his rear foot against the pitcher's rubber and then raises, or stretches, his hands above his head and brings them to a rest near his belt buckle before delivering the pitch. (The right foot is the rear foot for a right-handed pitcher, vice versa for a left-hander.) Pitchers usually work from the stretch when one or more runners are on base because, as the stretch involves less motion by the pitcher, he allows a runner less time to get a good jump on an ensuing steal attempt or base hit. See SET. Compare WINDUP.

v. To run for an additional base after hitting a ball, thus "stretching" the base hit from, say, a single into a double.

strike: n. 1. A pitch that passes through the strike zone and is not swung at by the batter; a pitch that the batter swings at and misses, regardless of its location in the strike zone; or a foul ball. Three strikes comprise an out, or a strike out, although a foul ball that is not a foul tip caught by the catcher while there are two strikes on the batter cannot be the third strike. See STRIKE OUT and STRIKE ZONE. 2. A perfect throw, as in, "The outfielder threw a strike to put out the baserunner at home plate."

strike out: n. A put out of the batter, recorded when he has made three strikes during an at-bat. The three-strikes-for-an-out rule was established in 1888. A strike out is recorded when, with two strikes, the batter swings at and misses a pitch; bunts the ball foul; hits a foul tip that the catcher holds; or fails to swing at a pitch in the strike zone. Also K and WHIFF. See STRIKE and STRIKE ZONE.

v. 1. To be put out by making a strike out. Also FAN and WHIFF. 2. To put out a batter by striking him out. Also FAN and WHIFF.

striker: n. A batter, in late-1800s baseball language.

strike zone: n. The imaginary rectangular area above home plate, through which a pitch must pass for the umpire to call it a strike. First established in 1887, the strike zone was set as the area above the plate between the top of the batter's shoulders and the bottom of his knees. It was changed to the area above the plate and between the batter's armpits and knee-tops in 1950, and then in 1963 changed back to the original dimensions. After the so-called Year of the Pitcher in 1968, the strike zone was shrunk back to its 1950–62 dimensions in 1969 to give the batters an advantage. (Nonetheless, any hitter who has argued balls and strikes with an umpire will tell you that the strike zone is clearly defined only in the rule book.)

stroke: n. 1. A base hit. The word originated in the late 1800s. 2. A batter's swing.
    v. To hit a ball sharply.

strong up the middle: See UP THE MIDDLE.

stuff: n. A pitcher's repertoire of pitches. If he is throwing well during a game, he is said to have his "good stuff" or "great stuff." There is no such thing as "bad stuff," at least not in baseball.

submarine: n. A pitch thrown with an underhand whiplike motion. Until overhand pitching was allowed in 1884, the submarine motion was the most common type of delivery among pitchers. Great submarine pitchers, or "submariners," in modern times have included Elden Auker in the 1930s and 1940s, Ted Abernathy from the 1950s to the 1970s, and Kent Tekulve and Dan Quisenberry in the 1970s and 1980s. Also CURVING UPSHOOT.
    v. To throw a submarine pitch.

sub, substitute: n. A nonstarting reserve player, who generally enters games to substitute for a teammate.

suicide squeeze: See SQUEEZE PLAY.

sun field: n. The area of the field, particularly the outfield, where the sun shines in the fielder's eyes.

suspended game: n. A game that is stopped, usually because of darkness or inclement weather, and will be completed at a later date.

swat: n. A batted ball that travels a great distance, especially a home run. The great slugger Babe Ruth was known as "The Sultan of Swat."

sweep: v. To win each game in a regular or postseason series.
   n. The winning of every game in a series.

sweetheart: n. A player who quietly and consistently does a solid job, and is respected by teammates and opponents alike as a true professional.

sweet spot: n. The area of a bat with which a batter best likes to make contact when swinging at a pitch, usually the head of the bat. The phrase also describes the area of the ball on which the batter likes to place the bat's "sweet spot." When he does, the result is usually a sharply hit line drive or a prodigious home run.

swing: v. To attempt to hit a pitch with the bat. If the batter swings and misses the ball, he is charged with a strike. Also CUT.
   n. An attempt to hit a pitch with the bat. Also CUT.

swinger: n. The batter.

swing for the downs, swing for the fences: v. To take wide and powerful swings at a pitch in the hope of hitting it out of the ballpark for a home run. "Downs" are elevated plateaus of land, so a ball that's hit to the downs would truly be a mighty blow.

swing from the heels: v. To take a wide and powerful swing at a pitch, an action that many batters take while shifting their weight to their heels.

swinging bunt: n. A slow, buntlike ground ball that the batter makes by taking a full swing but barely touching the ball.

swing man: See LONG MAN, LONG RELIEVER.

switch hit: v. To be able to bat from both the right and left sides of home plate.

switch hitter: n. A player who can bat both right-handed and left-handed. Most baseball historians agree that Mickey Mantle of the New York Yankees, with his combination of power and average, was the game's greatest switch hitter.

table is set, the: An expression meaning the bases are loaded. In other words, the "table is set" for the batter to drive in some runs.

tag: v. 1. To put out a baserunner by touching him with the hand, either the gloved or bare hand, that is holding the ball. Also TAG OUT. 2. To hit a ball hard. 3. See TAG UP.
n. The act of putting out a baserunner by tagging him or the base that he is approaching.

tag out: See TAG (v.1).

tag up: v. To prepare to advance on a fly ball by standing on a base and then running toward the next base only after the fielder has caught the ball. A batter is credited with a sacrifice fly and no time at bat only when a baserunner tags up and scores from third base. Also TAG.

tailing fastball: n. A fastball that makes a slight break away from the batter as the ball crosses home plate.

take: v. To let a pitch go by without swinging at it.

"Take Me Out to the Ball Game": n. The most famous song written about baseball, composed in the early 1900s by Jack Norworth. It is safe to say that even those Americans who do not consider themselves fans of the national pastime are familiar with the song's melody and some of its lyrics:

"Take me out to the ball game,
"Take me out to the crowd.
"Buy me some peanuts and Cracker jack.
"I don't care if I never get back.
"So let's root, root, root for the home team.
"If they don't win, it's a shame,
"For it's one, two, three strikes, you're out
"At the old ball game."

take one for the team: v. While batting, to intentionally allow oneself to be hit by a pitch. By doing so, the batter has helped his club by reaching first base, keeping an inning alive, and possibly advancing other baserunners. See HIT BY THE PITCH.

take out: v. To slide into an infielder with the intention of knocking him down. A "take out slide" is usually aimed at an infielder who has just forced out the baserunner and is attempting to complete a double play by throwing the ball to another base. "Taking out" the fielder sometimes prevents him from completing the double play.

take sign: n. A signal from a coach instructing a batter not to swing at the next pitch.

take something off a pitch: v. To throw a change-up, especially after giving the batter a steady diet of fastballs. What the pitcher takes off the pitch is speed.

take the ball deep, take the ball downtown: v. To hit a home run.

take the pitcher deep, take the pitcher downtown: v. To hit a home run.

tally-ho: n. A common practice of the early 1900s, in which ballplayers, dressed in their uniforms, rode in horse-drawn carriages to the ballpark of whatever town they were visiting. Clubhouses were rare in those days, especially for visiting teams, so players would dress at their hotel and ride to the park. The invention of National League player–manager Cap Anson, the "tally-ho" was usually an event in each town. Fans would tag along and hurl insults and sometimes rotten fruit at the visiting ballplayers. More than a few modern fans would not mind seeing this custom revived.

tape-measure home run: n. A home run hit such a long distance that it deserves to be measured. The practice started after Mickey Mantle of the New York Yankees hit a tremendous homer off Washington Senator pitcher Chuck Stobbs in 1953. Yankee public relations director Red Patterson later found a witness who saw where the ball landed. Patterson measured the shot at an incredible 565 feet.

tapper: n. A ground ball that travels at slow to medium speed. The name comes from the weak "tap" that the hitter apparently gave the ball with his bat.

tarp, tarpaulin: n. A large nylon covering placed over the diamond portion of the field after games and during rain delays. When not in use, the tarpaulin is rolled onto a long steel tube and set in foul territory. The first tarpaulin was made of canvas and introduced in 1889 by Abner Powell, the player–manager of a minor league team in New Orleans.

tater: n. A home run. The expression started among Negro League players as "long potatoes," was later shortened to "long tater," and popularized during the 1960s by George Scott of the Boston Red Sox. It was shortened even more to its present and best known form, "tater."

Temple Cup Series: n. A forerunner of the World Series, in which the first- and second-place teams in the National League played a best-of-seven series from 1894 to 1897 and once more in 1900 for the honor of winning a cup named after the series' creator, former Pittsburgh Pirate owner William Chase Temple.

Texas leaguer: n. A fly ball that falls just beyond the reach of the infielders and in front of the outfielders for a base hit. Also BLOOP, BLOOPER, DYING QUAIL, FLARE, LOOPER, QUAIL, QUAIL SHOT, and WOUNDED DUCK. The term dates back to 1890, when a player named Art Sunday was acquired by the Toledo team of the International League. Sunday, formerly a player on a Texas League club, became known for lofting soft fly balls for hits. A Toledo sportswriter once noted that Sunday struck "another of those Texas league hits."

third, third base: n. 1. The base on the left field foul line, 90 feet from home plate, and which must be touched by the runner as he advances from second base to home plate. Also FAR CORNER and HOT CORNER. 2. The position played by the third baseman. 3. A nickname for the third baseman.

third-base coach: n. A coach for the batting team who stands in the coach's box in foul territory near third base. His responsibilities include relaying signals from the manager to the batter and to baserunners, and deciding whether to "wave on" a runner to the next base.

third baseman: n. The infielder who positions himself near third base. Also THIRD, THIRD BASE.

three-bagger, three-base hit: n. A triple.

three-two pitch: n. A pitch thrown with a count of three balls and two strikes. Also PAY-OFF PITCH.

three up, three down: An expression meaning that the first three batters in an inning all made outs. Also ONE-TWO-THREE. See MOW DOWN, SET DOWN, and SKUNK.

through the wicket: prep. phrase. Through a fielder's legs. This expression, which is borrowed from cricket, is used when a fielder fails to scoop a ground ball and allows it to pass through his legs.

thrower: n. A pitcher who tries to get batters out by throwing little else but fastballs, as opposed to a "pitcher" who relies on finesse and an array of pitches delivered at various speeds. Also POWER PITCHER, Compare CONTROL PITCHER and FINESSE PITCHER.

throw ground balls: v. To throw pitches, usually low breaking balls, that result in the batters' hitting ground balls.

throw out: v. 1. To put out a baserunner by throwing the ball to another fielder, who then tags the runner or forces him at a base. 2. See EJECT.

throw out the first ball: v. To do the honorary act of throwing a ball to the home team's catcher, usually before an important game, such as an Opening Day, All-Star, play-off, or World Series contest. The custom is believed to have started when United States President William Howard Taft threw out the first ball at a Washington Senator home opener on April 14, 1910. (This is the same game at which Taft is said to have begun the practice of standing and stretching during the seventh inning of a game. See SEVENTH-INNING STRETCH.) Since then, nearly every U.S. President has thrown out a first ball, and the honor has long since been passed along to everyone from politicians to former stars of the home team to prominent local citizens.

thumb: See EJECT.

ticket: n. A base on balls, from FREE TICKET.

tight: adj. Close to the batter's body. The term is generally used to describe pitches.

time, timeout: n. A signal from one of the four umpires that play will temporarily stop, in which case the ball becomes "dead." The umpire may do so on his own, or on request by a player, coach, or manager. Only the home plate umpire can signal when play may be resumed.

Tinker-to-Evers-to-Chance: n. The most famous double-play combination in baseball history, consisting of shortstop Joe Tinker, second baseman Johnny Evers, and first baseman Frank Chance. The threesome probably owed their renown as much to the mellifluous sound of their names as to their sharp play. Regulars for the Chicago Cubs from 1903 to 1910, the three even inspired New York columnist Franklin P. Adams to write the following verse, "Baseball's Sad Lexicon," almost as well-known a piece of baseball poetry as "Casey at the Bat":

> "These are the saddest of possible words:
>   " 'Tinker to Evers to Chance.'
> "Trio of bear Cubs and fleeter than birds,
>   " 'Tinker to Evers to Chance.'
> "Ruthlessly pricking our gonfalon bubble,
> "Making a Giant hit into a double—
> "Words that are heavy with nothing but trouble:
>   " 'Tinker to Evers to Chance.' "

Though the trio worked in harmony on the field, there was discord between Joe Tinker and Johnny Evers off the diamond. On September 14, 1905, Evers took a taxi from the team's hotel to an exhibition game in Washington, Indiana, leaving his teammates behind in the lobby. Tinker brought the matter up later, the two men argued and had a fistfight on the field during the game. Throughout the rest of their careers, they barely spoke to each other.

tomahawk: v. To swing up at a pitch, particularly at a high pitch, with much the same motion of someone wielding a tomahawk. (It would be nice to report that a batter from the

Cleveland Indians or the Boston Braves invented this swinging motion, but alas, there is no way of knowing.)

tools: n. The abilities to hit for a high average, hit with power, run well, throw well, and field well. Not all ballplayers have each of these skills, but the men who do are said to have "all the tools." As Leo Durocher once put it, "There are only five things you can do in baseball—run, throw, catch, hit, and hit with power."

tools of ignorance: n. The equipment worn by the catcher, which includes a face mask, a chest protector, and shin guards. Muddy Ruel, a major league catcher from 1915 to 1934, coined the term, implying that only an "ignorant" person would be willing to withstand the physical punishment that befalls a catcher.

top: v. To swing at a pitch and hit the top of the ball, usually causing it to take a high bounce. See TOPPER.

top of the inning: n. The first half of an inning, during which the visiting team bats.

top of the order: n. The first three batters in the starting lineup (or those batters that may replace them and take their batting positions later in the game).

topper: n. A high bounding ground ball. Also BALTIMORE CHOP, BOUNDER, BUTCHER BOY, CHOP, and CHOPPER. See TOP.

toss: n. A throw or a pitch.
    v. 1. To make a throw or a pitch. 2. See EJECT.

tosser: n. A pitcher.

toss out: See EJECT.

total bases: n. The total number of bases that a batter or a team attains by base hits (a single equaling one base, a double two bases, a triple three bases and a home run four bases). So, if during one season a batter gets 20 home runs, 5 triples, 30 doubles, and 100 singles, his total bases for the year come to 255. That ain't hay, though it pales next to Babe Ruth's all-time season record of 457 total bases in 1921.

touch all the bases (touch 'em all): v. To step on, or "touch," each base after hitting a home run.

tough out: n. A batter who is difficult to put out, especially in a clutch situation. Compare EASY OUT and OUT MAN.

trap: v. To appear to catch a fly ball just above the ground, but actually to glove it immediately after the ball bounces on the ground.
　　　n. The act of trapping a ball in the glove.

triple: n. A batted ball that allows the batter to reach third base safely and without the benefit of fielding errors. Also THREE-BAGGER and THREE-BASE HIT.

Triple Crown: n. The achievement by one player of having the highest batting average, the most home runs and the most runs batted in for his league in a season. In 1878, Paul Hines of the National League Providence Club won the first Triple Crown in major league history with a .358 average, 4 home runs, and 50 runs batted in. Thirteen men have since turned the trick, the latest being the Boston Red Sox' Carl Yastrzemski in 1967 (.326, 44, 121).

tripleheader: n. Three games played consecutively on the same date. Only three tripleheaders have been staged in big league history, all of them in the National League. The first took place on September 1, 1890, as Pittsburgh swept Brooklyn by scores of 10–9, 3–2, and 8–4. On Septmeber 7, 1896, Baltimore took three from Louisville, 4–3, 9–1, and 12–1. The last triple-bill occurred on October 2, 1920, with Cincinnati beating Pittsburgh 13–4 and 7–3 in the first two games before dropping the finale 6–0.

triple play: n. A play in which three outs are made. Abbreviated TP. While triple plays are much rarer than double plays, several TPs usually occur each season.

triple steal: n. A play in which three baserunners simultaneously steal bases. This is a very rare play, though sometimes it works by its sheer shock effect on the defensive team.

triple up: v. To record the third and final out of a triple play.

turn around a fastball: v. To hit a fastball sharply, usually at a faster speed than at which it was thrown. For example, it is said of a line drive home run off a fastball that the ball "came in fast but it went out faster." Or "The batter turned that pitch around in a hurry."

turn the ball over: v. To throw a screwball. The term derives from the motion used by a pitcher while throwing a screwball, namely turning his hand, and thus the ball, over. See SCREWBALL.

turn the double play: v. To complete a double play. Usually the phrase applies to a double play in which both outs are made by putting out the runners at two bases. Also TURN TWO.

turn the pivot: v. To force a runner at second base and then, while the runner is sliding into the base, "pivot" and then throw the ball to first base to complete a double play. Also MAKE THE PIVOT.

turn two: See TURN THE DOUBLE PLAY.

tweener: n. A batted ball that goes between two outfielders and rolls to the outfield fence. Also GAPPER and GAP SHOT.

twin bill: See DOUBLEHEADER.

twi-night doubleheader, twi-nighter: n. A doubleheader that starts at twilight. See DOUBLEHEADER.

twin killing: See DOUBLE PLAY.

twirl: v. To pitch.

twirler: n. A pitcher.

two-bagger, two-base hit: See DOUBLE.

ump, umpire: n. An official who rules on plays during a ball game and is the final authority on a call. During a regular season game, an umpire is positioned behind or near each of the four bases, while during postseason games two extra umpires are stationed on each foul line in the outfield. The word, which was borrowed from cricket and rounders, derives from the Middle English "noumper," meaning a third party called in to mediate an argument between two persons. When the rules for modern baseball were first written in 1845, the word "umpire" was agreed on as the title of the game's officiator. The first professional umpire was a part-time boxer named William McLean, who earned five dollars a game in the National Association in 1871, the year that also saw the beginning of professional baseball. A second umpire was not used in major league games until the early 1900s. A third was added in the 1930s and a fourth in the 1950s. The practice of using six umpires in postseason play, with an ump on each foul line in the outfield, began in the mid-1950s. Also ARBITER.

umpire-in-chief: n. The umpire who positions himself behind the catcher and is the ultimate authority on how the game is conducted. Among his responsibilities are calling balls and strikes, deciding when games should be forfeited or halted because of inclement weather, and informing the official scorer of the starting lineups and any changes in the lineups during the game. Also BALL-AND-STRIKE UMPIRE, HOME PLATE UMPIRE and PLATE UMPIRE.

unassisted double play: n. A double play made by one player. For instance, when a first baseman catches a line drive and steps on first base after the runner has taken off on the hit without tagging up, then the first baseman is credited with making an unassisted double play.

unassisted put-out: n. A put-out made by a fielder who catches a fly ball or by a player in the infield who fields a ground ball and then steps on a base or tags a runner.

unassisted triple play: n. A triple play made by one player. One of baseball's rarest plays, the unassisted triple play has been made only eight times in major league history. The first was by Ned Ball of the Cleveland Indians in a 1909 game against the Boston Red Sox, while the last was by Washington Senator shortstop Ron Hansen against Cleveland in 1968.

Uncle Charlie: n. An excellent curve ball. The term's origin is uncertain.

unearned run: n. A run that is not credited to the pitcher when his earned run average is being tabulated. An unearned run is any run scored because of an error or catcher's interference, or any run scored after an error on a previous play that would have accounted for the final out of the inning. Compare EARNED RUN.

uni, uniform: n. A player's garb for a game, consisting of cleated shoes, stirrup sox, knickers, a pullover or buttoned shirt, and a cap. The first baseball team to wear a special uniform was the New York Knickerbockers, who in 1849 sported long pants similar to those worn by cricket players. The modern baseball uniform was introduced in 1868 by the Cincinnati Red Stockings, who wore knickered pants that initially drew much ridicule. The custom of wearing white uniforms at home and gray on the road was officially adopted in 1911, though Connie Mack reportedly introduced gray road uniforms even earlier. It seems that Mack's Philadelphia Athletics would not play so hard on the road because they felt bound to go all out only for the home fans and also because they failed to see the point of dirtying up their clean white uniforms by sliding and diving about the field. Mack thus ordered gray uniforms for road games, reasoning that his players would not mind soiling the darker outfits. Baseball uniforms were made of flannel until recent years when satin (an experiment during the early years of night games in the 1930s and 1940s) and double-knit, now the most common material, were introduced. Once Kansas City A's owner Charlie Finley dressed his players in bright green and yellow during the 1960s, various colors became the norm in baseball. Numbers on uniforms were not common until the New York Yankees started wearing large black numbers on their shirt backs in 1929. Other clubs had previously experimented with numbers, such as the Cincinnati Reds in 1888, the Cleveland Indians in 1916, and the St. Louis Cardinals in 1924 and 1925.

Union Association: n. One of the six "major" professional baseball leagues, founded in 1884 with 12 teams and lasting only that one season. The Union Association was organized by St. Louis millionaire Henry V. Lucas, who ignored baseball's reserve clause—the section of a player's contract that, until its abolition in the mid-1970s, tied him permanently to his club until he was released, sold, or traded—and lured many players from other big league teams. However, these teams merely lured the players back, and the association ended its only season with seven fewer clubs than it had started with.

up: adj. 1. At bat, as in the home plate umpire's familiar command, "Batter up!" 2. In a high section of, or above, the strike zone. Also UPSTAIRS.

upshoot: See RISING FASTBALL.

upstairs: See UP.

up the middle: adj. phrase. 1. Through the center of the infield toward center field, as in "There's a base hit up the middle." 2. Of or relating to the fielders who comprise the middle of the defensive alignment—catcher, shortstop, second baseman, and center fielder. A team with outstanding fielders at all of these positions is said to be "strong up the middle."

utility player: n. A nonstarting player who may be called on during a situation later in the game, when that particular player's special abilities as a pinch hitter, pinch runner, or defensive replacement are needed. "Utility player" is a euphemism for benchwarmer or reserve, much like "role player." Even so, journeyman utility man Kurt Bevacqua once said, "I hate the word 'utility.' It sounds like I work for the electric company."

velocity: n. The speed of a pitch. When a pitcher is said to be getting "good velocity," he is throwing outstanding fastballs.

vest-pocket catch: See BASKET CATCH.

visiting team, visitors: n. The team that travels to play in, or "visits," the opposing team in its home ball park. Because they are, after all, guests, the visitors are allowed to bat first, though this seeming courtesy can backfire in extra innings, when the home team automatically wins after breaking a tie with a score. If the visitors score in extra innings, they have to retire the home team before claiming the victory.

voodoo ball: n. A baseball that has been made with American parts but sewn in Haiti.

vultch: n. A save. The word comes from "vulture," and was hatched during the 1960s by starting pitchers who felt that relief pitchers all too often came into games and picked up easy saves after the starter had labored mightily through most of the contest. In the mid-1960s, Los Angeles Dodger reliever Phil Reagan was nicknamed "The Vulture" by his teammate, starting pitcher Claude Osteen. See SAVE.

wagon tongue: n. A bat. During the late 1800s, bats were made from old wagon tongues. In fact, bat manufacturers prized the hard seasoned wood that the old tongues provided.

waiter: n. A batter who waits patiently for a pitch that he knows he can best handle.

"Wait till next year": The battle cry of fans who, after suffering through a bad season by their favorite team, look optimistically to the upcoming year. The phrase is associated with the Brooklyn Dodger teams of the 1920s and 1930s, and was reportedly coined in 1871 by fans of the Brooklyn Eckfords, one of the charter member clubs of the National Association, baseball's first professional league.

walk: n. See BASE ON BALLS.
    v. 1. While pitching, to issue a base on balls. 2. While batting, to receive a base on balls.

walking lead: n. A lead in which the baserunner slowly takes a few steps off base while the pitcher makes his delivery to the plate. See LEAD.

Wally Pipp: n. A day off for a player. Pipp was the New York Yankees' veteran first baseman who, on June 1, 1925, de-

cided to take the day's game off because of a headache resulting from a beaning he received the day before. He was replaced by young Lou Gehrig. That was the first of Gehrig's
record 2,130 consecutive games as the Yanks' regular first
baseman. Poor Pipp never got his job back. A wag would later
observe that those were the most expensive aspirins Wally
Pipp ever took.

wand: See BAT.

war club: See BAT.

warm, warm up: v. To limber up the body by throwing or
stretching, either before or during a game. The terms are
often applied to relief pitchers throwing in the bullpen during a game in anticipation of entering the contest.

warm-up: n. The act of warming up.

warm-up pitches: n. The practice pitches made by a pitcher
between innings or by a relief pitcher when he enters a game
during an inning. A pitcher is allowed eight warm-up pitches at
the start of an inning or when he enters in relief during an
inning. When a pitcher must enter a game in an emergency—
for instance, when the previous pitcher has been suddenly
injured—and has not had sufficient time to warm up, then he
is allowed as many practice pitches as the plate umpire
deems necessary.

warning path, warning track: n. The area between the edge
of the outfield grass and the outfield fence. Made of dirt or
cinders, the track "warns" the outfielder, as he is running
back to make a play on a long fly ball, that he is nearing the
fence.

warning-track power: n. A somewhat derisive term for the
ability to hit a ball only as far as the warning track. In other
words, the batter is not strong enough to hit the ball over the
fence.

waste a pitch: v. To throw a pitch deliberately out of the strike zone while ahead of the batter in the count, thus setting up the next pitch, which will be intended to get out the batter. For example, when a pitcher has a count of no balls and two strikes on the batter, he may waste a pitch outside of the strike zone with the intention of throwing the next pitch inside to the batter for the third strike. Such a pitch is often called a "waste pitch." Sometimes the batter swings at and misses the waste pitch, which the pitcher does not mind at all.

wave the runner on: v. To signal to an advancing baserunner, by waving an arm in a windmill motion, to continue moving around the bases. Waving runners on is usually the duty of the third-base coach.

wax: v. To hit a ball hard.

web, webbing: n. The laced part of the fielding glove between the thumb and index finger. See FIELDING GLOVE.

wheelhouse: n. The area of the strike zone, usually chest high, in which a batter can best handle a pitch and hit it a long distance. When a batter hits a ball with power, he is said to have gotten the pitch "right in his wheelhouse."

wheels: n. A player's legs. A player who can run fast has "good wheels." A slow runner has "bad wheels" or, even worse, "no wheels."

whiff: n. A strike out, especially one made when the batter swings at and misses a pitch for the third strike. Thus he fans, or "whiffs," the air.
v. 1. To strike out while batting. 2. To strike out a batter.

whip: n. 1. A throwing arm. 2. A light bat, which the batter can easily "whip around."
v. To throw the ball with great velocity.

whitewash: n. A shutout, so called because it leaves the scoreless team's side of the scoreboard untainted by runs. The word is reported to have been first used in Connecticut baseball circles in the late 1860s. Also CHICAGO, KALSO-MINE, and SHUTOUT.

v. To shut out the opposing team. Also BLANK and CHICAGO.

wide: adj. Outside of the strike zone, as in "The first pitch is wide; ball one."

n. A pitch out of the strike zone. The term was used in this context during the 1800s.

wig-wag: v. To shake the bat, either nervously or ominously, while standing at the plate and awaiting the pitch.

wild: adj. Lacking control, unable to throw pitches for strikes. Also ALL OVER THE PLATE and SCATTER-ARMED.

wild pitch: n. A pitch that bounces away from the catcher and allows the baserunner or baserunners to advance, and is ruled the pitcher's fault. Compare PASSED BALL.

wild-pitch the runner to a base: v. To throw a wild pitch that allows a runner to advance a base.

willow: n. A bat. During the 1800s, bats were made from the light wood of the willow tree, thus allowing the hitter to swing with great speed at each pitch. The material was outlawed in the 1890s, however, when the baseball powers ruled that bats had to be made from harder wood. See BAT.

win: n. A victory credited to a pitcher's record. A win is awarded to a pitcher who starts a game and completes it with his team in the lead; a pitcher who starts a game, pitches at least five full innings, leaves with his team in the lead—a lead that must be maintained if that pitcher is to get the win; or a relief pitcher who enters a game with his team tied or behind, and who is still the pitcher of record when his team goes ahead in the contest and maintains that lead until the end of the game. (The exception to this rule occurs when a relief pitcher who has been ineffective is the pitcher of record when his team goes ahead. If another relief pitcher succeeds him and pitches well, then the official scorer may decide to give the win to the second pitcher.) Compare LOSS.

wind-blown home run: n. A fly ball that falls beyond the outfield fence with a good deal of assistance from a stong wind. Many pitchers, after giving up home runs, like to blame the wind for pushing the ball over the fence. During the 1984 season, a Seattle Mariner hurler called a shot hit off him a wind-blown homer, perhaps forgetting that he had been playing inside the covered Seattle Kingdome.

wind up: v. To swing the arms above the shoulders while delivering a pitch from the windup position.

windup: n. One of the two legal pitching deliveries, the other being the stretch. In the windup, the pitcher places his pivot foot atop the pitching rubber while facing the batter. He then delivers the pitch by taking one short backward step, swinging his gathered hands over his head, stepping forward while pushing off the rubber with his pivot foot, and then throwing the ball toward home plate. Compare SET and STRETCH.

wing: n. An arm, especially a pitcher's arm.
v. To make a throw or a pitch that has great velocity.

winning percentage: n. A statistic that measures what percentage of total games a team or a pitcher has won. To figure that stat, take the team's total number of games or a pitcher's total number of games in which he has gained a decision, and divide that number into the team's or the pitcher's number of wins. For example, a team that has won 12 of its 20 games has a winning percentage of .600. A pitcher who has won 5 of the

9 games in which he has gained a decision has a winning percentage of .556.

winning pitcher: See WIN.

winter ball: n. Baseball played by major league and minor league players during the winter off-season in organized leagues in foreign countries. Most winter ball is played in Caribbean countries.

wolves: n. Fans who are abusive of the players, showering them with either strong language or such objects as food, drink and, in the case of outfielder Dave Parker while he was playing in his home park in Pittsburgh, batteries.

wood: n. 1. Contact of the bat on the ball. When a batter makes solid contact with a pitch, he is said to have gotten "good wood on the ball." 2. A bat.

wooden Indian: n. A batter who takes a third strike. He does not swing his bat, standing as motionless as a cigar store wooden Indian. Also STATUE OF LIBERTY.

wood man: n. A good hitter. The phrase sometimes carries a negative connotation, suggesting that the player is not a good fielder but remains in the lineup because he handles the "wood," or the bat, well.

woodpile: See BAT RACK.

World Series: n. The best-four-of-seven-games series between the champions of the National and American Leagues, held at the end of each baseball season, to determine the World Champion. The first World Series was played in 1903 between the Boston Pilgrims of the American League and the Pittsburgh Pirates of the National League. The Pilgrims of the upstart "junior circuit" beat the Pirates five games to three in a best-five-of-nine Series, a format that was used again in the

WOLVES

Series from 1919 through 1921 before the seven-game set was permanently established. When John McGraw's New York Giants won the National League pennant in 1904, they refused to play the American League representative—Boston again—so no Series was played that year. However, the feud was patched up, the World Series was resumed the following year and has been held every season since then. (One might ask, just for the sake of semantics, how the American major leaguers can claim that their title series is for the "world" championship when there are now nearly 100 nations playing baseball. Nonetheless, baseball observers from Boston to Tokyo to Barcelona would agree that the best ball in the world is played in the United States, so it is not too farfetched to assert that the best professional team in America is the best team on the planet, or the "World Champions.") Also FALL CLASSIC, SERIES, and WORLD'S SERIOUS. See BRUSH RULES, THE.

World's Serious: n. The World Series. The term usually is said to have been coined by baseball reporter and short story writer Ring Larder in the early 1910s. However, sportswriter Fred Lieb wrote that the first person he heard use the phrase was Josh Devore, a New York Giant outfielder of that period. The expression, though somewhat comical in intent, reflected the seriousness with which the players and spectators of his day took the Series. The Fall Classic, in fact, remains a fairly intense affair for participants and observers alike.

wormburner: n. A sharply hit ground ball that stays close to the ground, thus scorching any worm unfortunate enough to be in the ball's path.

wormkiller: n. A ground ball whose first bounce sharply strikes the dirt near home plate. Should a worm be there, he wouldn't have a prayer.

wounded duck: n. A pop fly that travels on a low arc, landing with something of a thud, much like a duck that has been winged by a gun shot. Also DYING QUAIL.

wraparound swing: n. A swing in which the batter violently lashes at a pitch and, through the momentum of his motion, wraps his arms around himself. This most often occurs when a hitter, usually a slugger accustomed to taking powerful cuts, makes such a swing and misses the ball.

wrong field: See OFF FIELD.

yakker: n. A sharply breaking curve ball. The name is said to derive from the yawker, a kind of woodpecker whose curving path of flight is like that of a breaking ball.

yan: See YANNIGAN.

yank: v. To remove a player, especially a pitcher, from a game. When a manager "yanks" a pitcher, he gives him the "hook." See HOOK.

yannigan: A rookie. Jerry Denny, an infielder in the National League from 1881 to 1894, is credited with coining the term, reportedly taking it from the "yannigan bag," a carpetbag used by men whose jobs involved much traveling and were considered low-class occupations, such as prospectors and baseball players. Also YAN.

yellow hammer: n. A sharply breaking curve ball, named after a type of woodpecker that travels in an undulating manner resembling a curve ball.

"You can look it up": n. The famous utterance, usually attributed to Casey Stengel, implying that nearly every event and statistic of modern baseball history has been recorded and is available to anyone with enough curiosity and energy to dig up the appropriate source of information. While this quote has been attributed to humorists James Thurber (who wrote an uproarious baseball story titled "You Could Look It Up" that reportedly inspired Bill Veeck to use midget Eddie Gaedel as a pinch-hitter during an official major league game in 1951) and Ring Lardner, most experts agree that Casey was the true author. Sportswriter Harold Rosenthal reports that he first noticed the expression, and Stengel's use of it, in the mid-1950s. Only, Rosenthal adds, Stengel said it, "You kin look it up."

BIBLIOGRAPHY

My sources for this book ranged from friends of mine who happen to be baseball fanatics, sportswriters of my acquaintance, the special insights of Messrs. Barber, Barney, Creamer, and Rosenthal, and the approximately 25 years I've spent watching, listening to, reading about, and just plain pondering the Grand Old Game. Books that I found particularly helpful to my research are listed below:

Ahrens, Art, and Gold, Eddie. *Day by Day in Chicago Cubs History* (West Point, New York: Leisure Press, 1982).

Alexander, Charles C. *Ty Cobb* (New York: Oxford University Press, 1984).

Bouton, Jim, and Shecter, Leonard. *Ball Four* (New York: World Publishing Company, 1970).

Bready, James H. *The Home Team* (Baltimore: privately published, 1979).

Castillo, Carlos, and Bond, Otto F. *The University of Chicago Spanish Dictionary* (Chicago: The University of Chicago Press, 1948).

Chadwick, Henry. *How to Play Baseball* (Chicago: A.G. Spalding and Brothers, 1889).

Chieger, Bob. *Voices of Baseball: Quotations on the Summer Game* (New York: Atheneum, 1983).

Clark, Patrick. *Sports Firsts* (New York: Facts on File, Inc., 1981).

Considine, Tim. *The Language of Sport* (New York: World Almanac, 1982).

Creamer, Robert W. *Babe: The Legend Comes to Life* (New York: Simon and Schuster, 1974).

————*Stengel* (New York: Simon & Schuster, 1984).

Dallaire, Pierre. *Glossary of Baseball Terms: English-French, French-English* (Montreal: CBC Enterprises/Les Enterprises Radio-Canada, 1984).

Davids, L. Robert. *Insider's Baseball* (New York: Charles Scribner's and Sons, 1983).

Einstein, Charles. *The Baseball Reader* (Philadelphia: Lippincott and Crowell, 1980).

Fleming, G.H. *The Dizziest Season: The Gashouse Gang Chases the Pennant* (New York: William Morrow and Company, 1984).

Frommer, Harvey. *Sports Roots* (New York: Atheneum, 1979).

Gardner, Martin. *The Annotated Casey at the Bat* (Chicago: The University of Chicago Press, 1984).

Gold, Eddie. *White Sox and Cubs Trivia Book* (Chicago: Follett, 1981).

Hall, Donald. *Fathers Playing Catch with Sons* (San Francisco: North Point Press, 1985).

Kerrane, Kevin. *Dollar Sign on the Muscle: The World of Baseball Scouting* (New York: Beaufort Books Inc., 1984).

Kiernan, Thomas. *The Miracle at Coogan's Bluff* (New York: Thomas Y. Crowell Company, 1975).

Levine, Peter. *A.G. Spalding and the Rise of Baseball* (New York: Oxford University Press, 1985).

Lewis, Alec. *The Quotable Quotations Book* (New York: Thomas Y. Crowell Company, 1980).

Lieb, Fred. *Baseball as I Have Known It* (New York: Grossett and Dunlap, 1977).

McGraw, John J. *My Thirty Years in Baseball* (New York: Arno Press Inc., 1974, from the 1923 Boni and Liveright edition).

Mathews, Mitford M. *A Dictionary of Americanisms* (Chicago: The University of Chicago Press, 1948).

Mathewson, Christy. *Pitching in a Pinch, or Baseball from the Inside* (New York: Stein and Day, 1977, from the 1912 Putnam edition).

Morris, William and Mary. *Morris Dictionary of Word and Phrase Origins* (New York: Harper and Row, 1977).

Official Baseball Rules (St. Louis: Sporting News, 1984).

Okrent, Daniel, and Lewine, Harris. *The Ultimate Baseball Book* (Boston: Houghton Mifflin Company, 1979).

Pei, Mario A., and Ramondino, Salvatore. *The New World Spanish-English and English-Spanish Dictionary* (New York: The World Publishing Company, 1968).

Quigley, Martin. *The Crooked Pitch: The Curveball in American Baseball History* (Chapel Hill, North Carolina: Algonquin, 1984).

Reichler, Joseph L. *The Baseball Encyclopedia* (New York: MacMillan, 1982).

Ritter, Lawrence S. *The Glory of Their Times* (New York: William Morrow and Company, 1984).

Schlossberg, Dan. *The Baseball Catalog* (Middle Village, New York: Jonathan David, 1983).

Seymour, Harold. *Baseball: The Golden Age* (New York: Oxford University Press, 1971).

Thorn, John, and Palmer, Pete. *The Hidden Game of Baseball* (New York: Doubleday, 1984).

Veeck, Bill, and Linn, Ed. *Veeck—As in Wreck* (New York: Ballantine Books, 1976).

Whiteford, Mike. *How to Talk Baseball* (New York: Dembner, 1983).

Woolf, Henry Bosley. *Webster's New Collegiate Dictionary* (Springfield, Massachusetts: G. & C. Merriam Company, 1977).

Yardley, Jonathan. *Ring: A Biography of Ring Lardner* (New York: Random House, 1977).